I'm convinced that the Bible is somehow powerfully simple and beautifully complex. Like a diamond viewed from different angles, Scripture continually confronts my heart in fresh ways. This Bible-study series offers insightful perspectives and gives its participants a refreshing opportunity to admire the character of God and be transformed by the truth of his Word. Our souls need to meander through the minutiae and metanarrative of the Bible, and the **Storyline Bible Studies** help us do both.

> **KYLE IDLEMAN,** senior pastor of Southeast Christian Church and bestselling author of *Not a Fan* and *One at a Time*

If you are longing for a breath of fresh air in your spiritual life, this study is for you. Kat Armstrong brings to life both familiar and less familiar Bible stories in such an engaging way that you can't help but see how the God of the past is also working and moving in your present. Through the captivating truths revealed in this series, you will discover more about God's faithfulness, be equipped to move past fear and disappointment, and be empowered to be who you were created to be. If your faith has felt mundane or routine, these words will be a refreshing balm to your soul and a guide to go deeper in your relationship with God.

> **HOSANNA WONG,** international speaker and bestselling author of *How (Not) to Save the World: The Truth about Revealing God's Love to the People Right Next to You*

We are watching a new wave of Bible studies that care about the Bible's big story, from Genesis to Revelation; that plunge Bible readers into the depths of human despair and show them the glories of the Kingdom God plans for creation; and that invite readers to participate in that story in all its dimensions—in the mountains and the valleys. Anyone who ponders these Bible studies will come to terms not only with the storyline of the Bible but also with where each of us fits in God's grand narrative. I heartily commend Kat's **Storyline Bible Studies.**

> **REV. CANON DR. SCOT MCKNIGHT,** professor of New Testament at Northern Seminary

T0020758

Kat Armstrong is an able trail guide with contagious enthusiasm! In this series, she'll take you hiking through Scripture to experience mountains and valleys, sticks and stones, sinners and saints. If you are relatively new to the Bible or are struggling to see how it all fits together, your trek with Kat will be well worth it. You might even decide that hiking through the Bible is your new hobby.

CARMEN JOY IMES, associate professor of Old Testament at Biola University and author of *Bearing God's Name: Why Sinai Still Matters*

Kat Armstrong takes you into the heart of Scripture so that Scripture can grow in your heart. The **Storyline Bible Studies** have everything: the overarching story of God's redemption, the individual biblical story's historical context, and the text's interpretation that connects with today's realities. Armstrong asks insightful questions that make the Bible come alive and draws authentically on her own faith journey so that readers might deepen their relationship with Jesus. Beautifully written and accessible, the **Storyline Bible Studies** are a wonderful resource for individual or group study.

LYNN H. COHICK, PHD, provost and dean of academic affairs at Northern Seminary

Christians affirm that the Bible is God's Word and provides God's life-giving instruction and encouragement. But what good is such an authoritative and valuable text if God's people don't engage it to find the help the Scriptures provide? Here's where Kat Armstrong's studies shine. In each volume, she presents Bible study as a journey through Scripture that can be transformational. In the process, she enables readers to see the overarching storyline of the Bible and to find their place in that story. In addition, Armstrong reinforces the essential steps that make Bible study life-giving for people seeking to grow in their faith. Whether for individuals, for small groups, or as part of a church curriculum, these studies are ideally suited to draw students into a fresh and invigorating engagement with God's Word.

WILLIAM W. KLEIN, PHD, professor emeritus of New Testament interpretation and author of *Handbook for Personal Bible Study: Enriching Your Experience with God's Word*

Kat has done two things that I love. She's taken something that is familiar and presented it in a fresh way that is understandable by all, balancing the profound with accessibility. And her trustworthy and constant approach to Bible study equips the participant to emerge from this study with the ability to keep studying and growing more.

MARTY SOLOMON, creator and executive producer of *The BEMA Podcast*

You are in for an adventure. In this series, Kat pulls back the curtain to reveal how intentionally God has woven together seemingly disconnected moments in the collective Bible story. Her delivery is both brilliant and approachable. She will invite you to be a curious sleuth as you navigate familiar passages of Scripture, discovering things you'd never seen before. I promise you will never read the living Word the same again.

JENN JETT BARRETT, founder and visionary of The Well Summit

Kat has done it again! The same wisdom, depth, humility, and authenticity that we have come to expect from her previous work is on full display here in her new **Storyline Bible Study** series. Kat is the perfect guide through these important themes and through the story of Scripture: gentle and generous on the one hand, capable and clear on the other. She is a gifted communicator and teacher of God's Word. The format of these studies is helpful too—perfect pacing, just the right amount of new information at each turn, with plenty of space for writing and prayerful reflection as you go and some great resources for further study. I love learning from Kat, and I'm sure you will too. Grab a few friends from your church or neighborhood and dig into these incredible resources together to find your imagination awakened and your faith strengthened.

DAN LOWERY, president of Pillar Seminary

Kat Armstrong possesses something I deeply admire: a sincere and abiding respect for the Bible. Her tenaciousness to know more about her beloved Christ, her commitment to truth telling, and her desire to dig until she mines the deepest gold for her Bible-study readers makes her one of my favorite Bible teachers. I find few that match her scriptural attentiveness and even fewer that embody her humble spirit. This project is stunning, like the rest of her work.

LISA WHITTLE, bestselling author of *Jesus over Everything: Uncomplicating the Daily Struggle to Put Jesus First*, Bible teacher, and podcast host

MOUNTAINS

REDISCOVERING YOUR VISION AND
RESTORING YOUR HOPE IN GOD'S PRESENCE

KAT ARMSTRONG

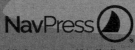

A NavPress resource published in alliance
with Tyndale House Publishers

NavPress ◖

NavPress is the publishing ministry of The Navigators, an international Christian organization and leader in personal spiritual development. NavPress is committed to helping people grow spiritually and enjoy lives of meaning and hope through personal and group resources that are biblically rooted, culturally relevant, and highly practical.

For more information, visit NavPress.com.

Mountains: Rediscovering Your Vision and Restoring Your Hope in God's Presence

Copyright © 2023 by Kat Armstrong. All rights reserved.

A NavPress resource published in alliance with Tyndale House Publishers

NavPress and the NavPress logo are registered trademarks of NavPress, The Navigators, Colorado Springs, CO. *Tyndale* is a registered trademark of Tyndale House Ministries. Absence of ® in connection with marks of NavPress or other parties does not indicate an absence of registration of those marks.

The Team: David Zimmerman, Publisher; Caitlyn Carlson, Editor; Elizabeth Schroll, Copy Editor; Olivia Eldredge, Operations Manager; Julie Chen, Designer; Sarah K. Johnson, Proofreader

Cover illustration by Lindsey Bergsma. Copyright © NavPress/The Navigators. All rights reserved.

Author photo by Judy Rodriquez, copyright © 2021. All rights reserved.

Author is represented by Jana Burson of The Christopher Ferebee Agency, christopherferebee.com

Some of the anecdotal illustrations in this book are true to life and are included with the permission of the persons involved. All other illustrations are composites of real situations, and any resemblance to people living or dead is purely coincidental.

For information about special discounts for bulk purchases, please contact Tyndale House Publishers at csresponse@tyndale.com, or call 1-855-277-9400.

ISBN 978-1-64158-580-4

Printed in the United States of America

29	28	27	26	25	24	23
8	7	6	5	4	3	2

For my dad, Ronald K. Obenhaus.
I think you would have loved this.

Contents

A Message from Kat

THE BIBLE IS a literary masterpiece.

Whether you are new to the Christian faith or a seasoned Bible reader, I wrote the **Storyline Bible Studies** to guide you through the story of Scripture—each following a person, place, or thing in the Bible. Maybe you are practiced in dissecting a passage or verse and pulling things out of the text to apply to your life. But now you may feel as though your faith is fragmented, coming apart at the seams. The **Storyline Bible Studies** will help you put things back together. You'll discover cohesive, thematic storylines with literary elements and appreciate the Bible as the literary masterpiece that it is.

Tracing a biblical theme, with imagery like mountains and valleys or sticks and stones, will spark your holy curiosity and empower you to cultivate a biblical imagination. I'm praying that your time studying God's Word is an awe-inspiring catalyst to engage and experience God's truth—that you would marvel at the artistry of God's storytelling. And that the Bible will never feel dull or boring ever again.

I wrote *Mountains* during a terribly painful season of isolation. I never doubted my faith in God, and thankfully I had dear friends loving me well. But I ached to experience God's nearness—his companionship. The global pandemic and its shutdowns, the polarizing political landscape, the rising racial tensions, and the insurrection at the Capitol were enough to make me despair, but being in vocational ministry during these fractures left me feeling very alone.

My prayer life was a broken record: *Wonderful Counselor, help!*

I needed to meet with God, desperately. I needed to hear his voice and imagine his loving, strong arms wrapped around me. That's what started me on a quest to study mountains in the Bible. I feel so close to God when I'm on a summit, drinking in the thin air.

As it turns out, the function mountains serve in my personal life—as a place to connect with my Savior—is the same function they serve in the Scriptures.

If you need God's presence, I wrote this study for you.

Love,

Kat

The Storyline of Scripture

YOUR DECISION TO STUDY THE BIBLE for the next few weeks is no accident—God has brought you here, to this moment. And I don't want to take it for granted. Here, at the beginning, I want to invite you into the most important step you can take, the one that brings the whole of the Bible alive in extraordinary ways: a relationship with Jesus.

The Bible is a collection of divinely inspired manuscripts written over fifteen hundred years by at least forty different authors. Together, the manuscripts make up tens of thousands of verses, sixty-six books, and two testaments. Point being: It's a lot of content.

But the Bible is really just one big story: God's story of redemption. From Genesis to Revelation the Bible includes narratives, songs, poems, wisdom literature, letters, and even apocalyptic prophecies. And yet, everything we read in God's Word helps us understand God's love and his plan to be in a relationship with us.

If you hear nothing else, hear this: God loves you.

It's easy to get lost in the vast amount of information in the Bible, so we're going to explore the storyline of Scripture in four parts. And as you locate your experience in the story of the Bible, I hope the story of redemption becomes your own.

PART 1: GOD MADE SOMETHING GOOD.

The big story—God's story of redemption—started in a garden. When God launched his project for humanity, he purposed all of us—his image bearers—to flourish and co-create with him. In the beginning there was peace, beauty, order, and abundant life. The soil was good. Life was good. We rarely hear this part of our story, but it doesn't make it less true. God created something good—and that includes you.

PART 2: WE MESSED IT UP.

If you've ever thought, *This isn't how it's supposed to be*, you're right. It's not. We messed up God's good world. Do you ever feel like you've won gold medals in messing things up? Me too. All humanity shares in that brokenness. We are imperfect. The people we love are imperfect. Our systems are jacked, and our world is broken. And that's on us. We made the mess, and we literally can't help ourselves. We need to be rescued from our circumstances, the systems in which we live, and ourselves.

PART 3: JESUS MAKES IT RIGHT.

The good news is that God can clean up all our messes, and he does so through the life, death, and resurrection of Jesus Christ. No one denies that Jesus lived and died. That's just history. It's the empty tomb and the hundreds of eyewitnesses who saw Jesus after his death that make us scratch our heads. Because science can only prove something that is repeatable, we are dependent upon the eyewitness testimonies of Jesus' resurrection for this once-in-history moment. If Jesus rose from the dead—and I believe he did—Jesus is exactly who he said he was, and he accomplished exactly what had been predicted for thousands of years. He restored us. Jesus made *it*, all of it, right. He can forgive your sins and connect you to the holy God through his life, death, and resurrection.

PART 4: ONE DAY, GOD WILL MAKE ALL THINGS NEW.

The best news is that this is not as good as it gets. A day is coming when Christ will return. He's coming back to re-create our world: a place with no tears, no pain, no suffering, no brokenness, no helplessness—just love. God will make all things new. In the meantime, God invites you to step into his storyline, to join him in his work of restoring all things. Rescued restorers live with purpose and on mission: not a life devoid of hardship, but one filled with enduring hope.

RESPONDING TO GOD'S STORYLINE

If the storyline of Scripture feels like a lightbulb turning on in your soul, that, my friend, is the one true, living God, who eternally exists as Father, Son, and Holy Spirit. God is inviting you into a relationship with him to have your sins forgiven and secure a place in his presence forever. When you locate your story within God's story of redemption, you begin a lifelong relationship with God that brings meaning, hope, and restoration to your life.

Take a moment now to begin a relationship with Christ:

God, I believe the story of the Bible, that Jesus is Lord and you raised him from the dead to forgive my sins and make our relationship possible. Your storyline is now my story. I want to learn how to love you and share your love with others. Amen.

If you confess with your lips that Jesus is Lord and believe in your heart that God raised him from the dead, you will be saved.

ROMANS 10:9, NRSV

How to Use This Bible Study

THE **STORYLINE BIBLE STUDIES** are versatile and can be used for

- ▲ individual study (self-paced),
- ▲ small groups (five or ten-lesson curriculum), or
- ▲ church ministry (semester-long curriculum).

INDIVIDUAL STUDY

Each lesson in the *Mountains* Bible study is divided into four fifteen- to twenty-minute parts (sixty to eighty minutes of individual study time per lesson). You can work through the material one part at a time over a few different days or all in one sitting. Either way, this study will be like anything good in your life: What you put in, you get out. Each of the four parts of each lesson will help you practice Bible-study methods.

SMALL GROUPS

Working through the *Mountains* Bible study with a group could be a catalyst for life change. Although the Holy Spirit can teach you truth when you read the Bible on your own, I want to encourage you to gather a small group together to work through this study for these reasons:

- God himself is in communion as one essence and three persons: Father, Son, and Holy Spirit.
- Interconnected, interdependent relationships are hallmarks of the Christian faith life.
- When we collaborate with each other in Bible study, we have access to the viewpoints of our brothers and sisters in Christ, which enrich our understanding of the truth.

For this Bible study, every small-group member will need a copy of the *Mountains* study guide. In addition, I've created a free downloadable small-group guide that includes

- discussion questions for each lesson,
- Scripture readings, and
- prayer prompts.

Whether you've been a discussion leader for decades or just volunteered to lead a group for the first time, you'll find the resources you need to create a loving atmosphere for men and women to grow in Christlikeness. You can download the small-group guide using this QR code.

CHURCH MINISTRY

Church and ministry leaders: Your work is sacred. I know that planning and leading through a semester of ministry can be both challenging and rewarding. That's why every **Storyline Bible Study** is written so that you can build modular semesters of ministry. The *Mountains* Bible study is designed to complement the

Valleys Bible study. Together, *Mountains* and *Valleys* can support a whole semester of ministry seamlessly, inviting the people you lead into God's Word and making your life simpler.

To further equip church and ministry leaders, I've created *The Leader's Guide*, a free digital resource. You can download *The Leader's Guide* using this QR code.

The Leader's Guide offers these resources:

- ▲ a sample ministry calendar for a ten-plus-lesson semester of ministry,
- ▲ small-group discussion questions for each lesson,
- ▲ Scripture readings for each lesson,
- ▲ prayer prompts for each lesson,
- ▲ five teaching topics for messages that could be taught in large-group settings, and
- ▲ resources for deeper study.

SPECIAL FEATURES

However you decide to utilize the *Mountains* Bible study, whether for individual, self-paced devotional time; as a small-group curriculum; or for semester-long church ministry, you'll notice several stand-out features unique to the **Storyline Bible Studies**:

- ▲ gospel presentation at the beginning of each Bible study;
- ▲ full Scripture passages included in the study so that you can mark up the text and keep your notes in one place;
- ▲ insights from diverse scholars, authors, and Bible teachers;
- ▲ an emphasis on close readings of large portions of Scripture;
- ▲ following one theme instead of focusing on one verse or passage;
- ▲ Christological narrative theology without a lot of church-y words; and
- ▲ retrospective or imaginative readings of the Bible to help Christians follow the storyline of Scripture.

You may have studied the Bible by book, topic, or passage before; all those approaches are enriching ways to read the Word of God. The **Storyline Bible Studies** follow a literary thread to deepen your appreciation for God's master plan of redemption and develop your skill in connecting the Old Testament to the New.

THE MOUNTAINS STORYLINE

I WAS SIPPING HOT CHOCOLATE and watching the sunrise with my husband, Aaron, and our son, Caleb, in a cozy cabin in Broken Bow, Oklahoma, when it dawned on me how many mountains are mentioned in the Bible. I'd been ruminating over some stories in Matthew's Gospel that all mention mountains, and it felt like someone had just pulled down on a lightbulb string and turned on my brain. Jesus was tempted on a mountain, he delivered his most famous sermon on a mountain, he was transfigured on a mountain, and he even gave his Great Commission on a mountain. Little did I know that this moment was the beginning of the **Storyline Bible Studies**.

I'd always been taught that the Bible was a cohesive and interconnected story, but frankly, I didn't believe it. On the surface, the Old and New Testaments seemed wildly different, and I rarely went beyond one single book of the Bible when I studied the Scriptures.

But the Gospel of Matthew is connected to the Old Testament, and the mountains in Genesis and Exodus carry symbolic meaning forward to mountains in the book of Matthew. Every mountain we survey in this Bible study is deeply embedded in an ancient, symbol-driven world where location didn't just matter—it had meaning. Sometimes God repurposes familiar settings to signal deeper significance. The *Mountains* Bible study will guide you through five mountaintop Bible stories because mountains symbolize places where God reveals his character and we can enjoy his presence.

In the Bible, several pivotal moments in our faith history take place on ancient mountains. As we will see, the location isn't incidental. Mountains are where God meets with his people. As one of God's preferred meeting spaces, mountains in the Bible take on symbolic meaning. Mountains are holy ground for connecting with God.

In *Mountains*, we're going to explore

- *Genesis 1–2*: the Mount of Creation, where God created the world;
- *Exodus 19–20*: Mount Sinai, where God gave the Israelites the Mosaic law;
- *Matthew 5*: the Mount of the Sermon, where Jesus delivered his most famous message;
- *Matthew 17*: the Mount of Transfiguration, where Jesus revealed his glory; and
- *Matthew 28*: the Mount of the Great Commission, where Jesus commissioned his disciples.

We're going to do this by looking at each mountain through four different lenses:

- **PART 1: CONTEXT.** Do you ever feel dropped into a Bible story disoriented? Part 1 will introduce you to the mountain you're going to study and its scriptural context. Getting your bearings before you read will enable you to answer the question *What am I about to read?*

▲ **PART 2: SEEING.** Do you ever read on autopilot? I do too. Sometimes I finish reading without a clue as to what just happened. A better way to read the Bible is to practice thoughtful, close reading of Scripture to absorb the message God is offering to us. That's why part 2 includes close Scripture reading and observation questions to empower you to answer the question *What is the story saying?*

▲ **PART 3: UNDERSTANDING.** If you've ever scratched your head after reading your Bible, part 3 will give you the tools to understand the author's intended meaning both for the original audience and for you. Plus you'll practice connecting the Old and New Testaments to get a fuller picture of God's unchanging grace. Part 3 will enable you to answer the question *What does it mean?*

▲ **PART 4: RESPONDING.** The purpose of Bible study is to help you become more Christlike; that's why part 4 will include journaling space for your reflection on and responses to the content and a blank checklist for actionable next steps. You'll be able to process what you're learning so that you can live out the concepts and pursue Christlikeness. Part 4 will enable you to answer the questions *What truths is this passage teaching?* and *How do I apply this to my life?*

One of my prayers for you, as a curious Bible reader, is that our journey through this study will help you cultivate a biblical imagination so that you're able to make connections throughout the whole storyline of the Bible. In each lesson, I'll do my best to include a few verses from different places in the Bible that are connected to our mountain stories. In the course of this study, we'll see the way God shows up on mountains throughout his Word—and get a glimpse of how he might show up in our lives today.

God's Word is so wonderful, I hardly know how to contain my excitement. Feel free to geek out with me; let your geek flag fly high, my friends. When we can see how interrelated all the parts of Scripture are to each other, we'll find our affection for God stirred as we see his artistic brilliance unfold.

BECOMING SECURE IN YOUR IDENTITY

MOUNT OF CREATION:
WHERE GOD LAUNCHES THE WORLD

SCRIPTURE: GENESIS 1–2

PART 1

CONTEXT

Before you begin your study, we will start with the context of the story we are about to read together: the setting, both cultural and historical; the people involved; and where our passage fits in the larger setting of Scripture. All these things help us make sense of what we're reading. Understanding the context of a Bible story is fundamental to reading Scripture well. Getting your bearings before you read will enable you to answer the question *What am I about to read?*

I'M AFRAID OF HEIGHTS, and I'm not the most outdoorsy person you've met. That's why my family is bewildered by my newfound love of hiking. For two decades of my marriage, vacation-Kat lounged poolside—and now (even though my skill level matches that of young children), I want to spend my summers hiking.

What happened? A mountaintop experience in Angel Fire, New Mexico.

On our way up the mountain, our feet dangling from the chairlift like dancing wind chimes, I turned to my husband, Aaron, to jokingly ask, "So, this is a mountain?" He spread out his arms like Vanna White on *Wheel of Fortune*, presenting the hillside in all its glory. "Wait till we get to the top, babe," he said.

At the top, Aaron suggested, we would find out what I was "really made of." He was right. Mountaintop experiences have a way of revealing the truth—the truth about ourselves and truths about God.

In our first lesson, we are going to study the story of Creation in the Garden of Eden, which takes place on top of a mountain. Yes, you read that right: Eden was on top of a mountain.

Why do I believe God's paradise to be in a raised position? Let's take a look at Ezekiel 28:11-16.

As you read, circle any time you notice God, through the prophet Ezekiel, equate Eden with God's holy mountain:

[11] The word of the LORD came to me: [12] "Son of man, take up a lament concerning the king of Tyre and say to him: 'This is what the Sovereign LORD says:

"'You were the seal of perfection,
    full of wisdom and perfect in beauty.
[13] You were in Eden,
    the garden of God;
every precious stone adorned you:
    carnelian, chrysolite and emerald,
    topaz, onyx and jasper,
    lapis lazuli, turquoise and beryl.
Your settings and mountings were made of gold;
    on the day you were created they were prepared.
[14] You were anointed as a guardian cherub,
    for so I ordained you.
You were on the holy mount of God;
    you walked among the fiery stones.
[15] You were blameless in your ways
    from the day you were created
    till wickedness was found in you.
[16] Through your widespread trade
    you were filled with violence,
    and you sinned.

So I drove you in disgrace from the mount of God,

    and I expelled you, guardian cherub,

    from among the fiery stones.'"

EZEKIEL 28:11-16

I realize that placing Eden on a mountain is a new concept to many of us—it certainly was for me. But there are solid reasons to understand it this way. In addition to the scriptural evidence in Ezekiel 28:11-16, we also know that in the Ancient Near Eastern culture mountains were considered holy—hinge points for heaven meeting earth.

On the *BibleProject Podcast*, Tim Mackie and Jon Collins summarize the "imaginative framework" most of the early readers of Genesis would have been filtering the Creation story through.[1] Many ancient kings built temples, places to live and worship, on mountains. In Greek mythology, Mount Olympus is home to the gods. Ancient readers would have readily envisioned Eden as a cosmic mountain.

In his book *The Tabernacle Pre-Figured: Cosmic Mountain Ideology in Genesis and Exodus*, biblical studies professor L. Michael Morales defines cosmic-mountain ideology this way:

> The mountain is sacred, the dwelling place of the gods, the intersection
> between heaven and earth, the central and highest place of the world . . . ,
> and the foundation and navel of creation.[2]

Morales's research shows that the idea of the cosmic mountain would have been fundamental to the ancient readings of the biblical narrative.[3] This understanding may be new to us, but when we combine the teaching of Scripture with the cultural context, I think we should imagine Eden on top of a mountain.

You are about to read your origin story. The first two chapters of God's story of redemption are about the Creator creating creation.[4] Although the Creation story is not written *to us*, it is most certainly *for us*. Modern Bible readers like you and me might have lingering questions when we read the Creation narrative because we know about dinosaurs and theories of the age of the earth. But the original audience of Genesis 1 and 2 read through a different lens, asked different questions, and lived in a different culture. As pastor and author Dan Kimball points out,

> God used what the people were familiar with to communicate the true creation story. In telling this story, God was not trying to communicate modern science to an ancient people, he was trying to communicate to the Israelites that he alone is God, the true God who created everything.[5]

I would add that God was also revealing who we are in light of our Creator—that he secured our identity to himself.

God's story begins not with a science lesson but with the truth that he is the only one *able* to create something from nothing—*and* that it was good.[7] This would have been a revolutionary way for God's people to understand their reality because, at the time Genesis was written, they were living as exiles, questioning God's faithfulness and plan. When Moses was inspired by the Holy Spirit to write and edit the Torah, the Israelites were suffering Egyptian slavery and mourning hundreds of years of unmet expectations. As God's chosen people, they had been promised a future full of land and blessings but were experiencing neither (Genesis 12).

Genesis introduces us to an awesome God who holds a good world in loving hands.[6]

Rodney S. Sadler Jr., "Genesis," in *The Africana Bible*

You've probably tried to reconcile the truth of a good God with circumstances that seem to communicate the opposite. Or the longing that fills your heart when years of unmet expectations shape your worldview. We tend to create alternative narratives to explain away our brokenness. I understand that. Times of testing really shake my confidence in God and cause me to question my identity as God's beloved. When I am disappointed in God's timing or frustrated by his plan, insecurities arise in me, causing me to question his care. *Does God care about me? Am I still a beloved child of God? If I'm not experiencing the blessings that come with being one of God's children, am I really his after all? And if not his beloved, who am I?*

See my downward spiral into doubt?

When doubt arises, we need something solid and true to ground us. Imagine with me listening to the Mount Eden story as a desperate Israelite questioning your identity. You look around and see how sideways life has become for your people and wonder, *How did we get here? Are we really God's people?*

Like our brothers and sisters from the past, we hear what they heard: that the sin and injustice around us are not God's doing—they're ours.[8] But we also hear this good news: There is only one true, living God who eternally exists as Father, Son, and Holy Spirit; and the creatures God creates have inherent dignity, worth, and value. We are designed to care for his creation, and we are defined by our relationship with our Creator.[9] The truths you learn in Genesis about your origin story have the power to make you unshakably confident in your identity as God's image bearer.

You are about to read a story not about cosmology but about covenant.[10]

1. **PERSONAL CONTEXT: What is going on in your life right now that might impact how you understand this Bible story?**

2. **SPIRITUAL CONTEXT: If you've never studied this Bible story before, what piques your curiosity? If you've studied this passage before, what are some things you remember being taught on the subject?**

SEEING

Seeing the text is vital if we want the heart of the Scripture passage to sink in. We read slowly and intentionally through the text with the context in mind. As we practice close, thoughtful reading of Scripture, we pick up on phrases, implications, and meanings we might otherwise have missed. Part 2 includes close Scripture reading and observation questions to empower you to answer the question *What is the story saying?*

1. **Read Genesis 1:1–2:3, and draw a box every time God creates.**

1 In the beginning God created the heavens and the earth. ² Now the earth was formless and empty, darkness was over the surface of the deep, and the Spirit of God was hovering over the waters.

³ And God said, "Let there be light," and there was light. ⁴ God saw that the light was good, and he separated the light from the darkness. ⁵ God called the light "day," and the darkness he called "night." And there was evening, and there was morning—the first day.

⁶ And God said, "Let there be a vault between the waters to separate water from water." ⁷ So God made the vault and separated the water under the vault from the water above it. And it was so. ⁸ God called the

vault "sky." And there was evening, and there was morning—the second day.

⁹ And God said, "Let the water under the sky be gathered to one place, and let dry ground appear." And it was so. ¹⁰ God called the dry ground "land," and the gathered waters he called "seas." And God saw that it was good.

¹¹ Then God said, "Let the land produce vegetation: seed-bearing plants and trees on the land that bear fruit with seed in it, according to their various kinds." And it was so. ¹² The land produced vegetation: plants bearing seed according to their kinds and trees bearing fruit with seed in it according to their kinds. And God saw that it was good. ¹³ And there was evening, and there was morning—the third day.

¹⁴ And God said, "Let there be lights in the vault of the sky to separate the day from the night, and let them serve as signs to mark sacred times, and days and years, ¹⁵ and let them be lights in the vault of the sky to give light on the earth." And it was so. ¹⁶ God made two great lights—the greater light to govern the day and the lesser light to govern the night. He also made the stars. ¹⁷ God set them in the vault of the sky to give light on the earth, ¹⁸ to govern the day and the night, and to separate light from darkness. And God saw that it was good. ¹⁹ And there was evening, and there was morning—the fourth day.

²⁰ And God said, "Let the water teem with living creatures, and let birds fly above the earth across the vault of the sky." ²¹ So God created the great creatures of the sea and every living thing with which the water teems and that moves about in it, according to their kinds, and every winged bird according to its kind. And God saw that it was good. ²² God blessed them and said, "Be fruitful and increase in number and fill the water in the seas, and let the birds increase on the earth." ²³ And there was evening, and there was morning—the fifth day.

²⁴ And God said, "Let the land produce living creatures according to their kinds: the livestock, the creatures that move along the ground,

and the wild animals, each according to its kind." And it was so. ²⁵ God made the wild animals according to their kinds, the livestock according to their kinds, and all the creatures that move along the ground according to their kinds. And God saw that it was good.

²⁶ Then God said, "Let us make mankind in our image, in our likeness, so that they may rule over the fish in the sea and the birds in the sky, over the livestock and all the wild animals, and over all the creatures that move along the ground."

²⁷ So God created mankind in his own image,
    in the image of God he created them;
    male and female he created them.

²⁸ God blessed them and said to them, "Be fruitful and increase in number; fill the earth and subdue it. Rule over the fish in the sea and the birds in the sky and over every living creature that moves on the ground."

²⁹ Then God said, "I give you every seed-bearing plant on the face of the whole earth and every tree that has fruit with seed in it. They will be yours for food. ³⁰ And to all the beasts of the earth and all the birds in the sky and all the creatures that move along the ground—everything that has the breath of life in it—I give every green plant for food." And it was so.

³¹ God saw all that he had made, and it was very good. And there was evening, and there was morning—the sixth day.

2 Thus the heavens and the earth were completed in all their vast array.

² By the seventh day God had finished the work he had been doing; so on the seventh day he rested from all his work. ³ Then God blessed the seventh day and made it holy, because on it he rested from all the work of creating that he had done.

GENESIS 1:1–2:3

2. According to Genesis 1:26-27, what does every human share with God?

Remember, God called you good—very good, in fact. You may not feel like you are good or have the faith to believe it, but being made in God's image and reflecting his likeness is the truest thing about you. He created you so he could be in a relationship with you, and that relationship doesn't change based on your actions.

3. According to Genesis 1:28, what purpose did God give Adam and Eve?

Adam and Eve were designated as vice-regents of the world, and every one of us inherits that calling too. We will not find our purpose in a relationship status, a role within our family, or a title at work, although all those things can be gifts from God. They may be an avenue for us to exercise our purpose—but our purpose is the same as Adam and Eve's—to be God's representatives in this world, and to see to it that the world, and everything and everyone in it, flourishes.

What happens next, in Genesis 3, is an epic failure on Adam and Eve's part. They rebel against God's instructions to stay away from the tree of the knowledge of good and evil, choosing autonomy instead of finding freedom and assurance as image bearers of God. Adam and Eve try to be like God in a way that is not good for them.

As a result, God drives Adam and Eve out of Eden. Keep in mind the imagery of Eden on a mountaintop. Adam and Eve were not just walking away from a garden—they had to journey down the side of a mountain. Their expulsion is a type of exile from God's presence, and their physical distance from Mount Eden symbolized a relational distance between God and his people. This painful separation would continue until another mountaintop revelation, which we'll get to in our next lesson.

4. **Imagine what Adam and Eve must have been experiencing as they climbed down from God's paradise. List out what things may have come to their minds as they climbed down Mount Eden. You may want to read Genesis 3 to help imagine their internal processing.**

▲

▲

▲

▲

After Adam and Eve's descent from Eden, God placed cherubim and a fiery sword to guard the garden (Genesis 3:24). Cherubim in the Bible are heavenly creatures, likely scary angelic figures, that served as the "connection point between the heavens and earth."[11] Biblical and theological studies professor Dru Johnson summarizes the significance the cherubim represent in this story: "The *cherubim* guarding Eden represent more than armed guards. They signal the beginning of God's presence drawn back to the heavens, and a mediated presence on earth through symbols and messengers/angels."[12] Cherubim were the hinge on the gate to God.

Maybe you've heard the Adam and Eve story told as "the Fall" of mankind. No truer words could describe the separation their sin caused all of us. Adam and Eve's rebellion against God's clear instructions was a fall from God's presence, a fall from an intimate relationship with him, and a fall from the mountain where he lived. We should feel the tense reality in this story: There seems to be no coming back from this fall from grace.

But the separation between God and his people would not be forever. The Scriptures point to a redemption of Adam and Eve's fall from Mount Eden through Jesus Christ.

PART 3

UNDERSTANDING

Now that we've finished a close reading of the Scriptures, we're going to spend some time on interpretation: doing our best to understand what God was saying to the original audience and what he's teaching us through the process. But to do so, we need to learn his ways and consider how God's Word would have been understood by the original audience before applying the same truths to our own lives. "Scripture interpretation" may sound a little stuffy, but understanding what God means to communicate to us in the Bible is crucial to enjoying a close relationship with Jesus. Part 3 will enable you to answer the question *What does it mean?*

MY NEPHEW BARRETT is three years old and the cutest little nugget you've ever wanted to snuggle. During the global pandemic, I had the privilege of extra time with him—and as a result, I learned to "speak Barrett." At first, it was a challenge to understand what he wanted, but through some toddler trials and auntie errors, we figured it out. Barrett likes access to water at all times. He likes mac and cheese, and he does *not* like mosquitoes. Once I learned how to interpret some of his cues, we found a whole new level of closeness.

Interpretation means paying attention to how someone is communicating so we can understand and know them better. One simple method for figuring out God's intended meaning in age-old stories is to put ourselves in the original audience's shoes, to imagine how they would have heard the story and how it would have changed their lives. The chart below will help you practice just that. You may want to reread Genesis 1:1–2:3 to fill in the blanks.

1. Fill out the chart below, including the two blank rows.

What did you learn about God in Genesis 1:1–2:3?	How would this have encouraged the ancient Israelites?	How does this truth encourage you?
God lives in a holy mountain.		
God is holy.		
God is the Creator who creates creatures.		
God completes his work.		

On Mount Eden, God reveals to us that he is accessible, relational, creative, and intentional. He starts projects, and he finishes them too. Praise God! Because you and I are works in progress.

2. **What is something in your life that comes to mind when you think about being a work in progress?**

MAKING CONNECTIONS

An important part of understanding the meaning of a Bible passage is getting a sense of its place in the broader storyline of Scripture. When we make connections between different parts of the Bible, we get a glimpse of the unity and cohesion of the Scriptures.

In the book of Ephesians, we find a connection between the redemption God *initiated* at Creation in Genesis and the redemption he *will bring to completion* when Christ returns and creates the new heaven and new earth. Under the inspiration of the Holy Spirit, the apostle Paul authored a letter to the Christians living in Ephesus, and in it he alluded to the Creation story. The Christians in Ephesus were mid–identity crisis, much like the Israelites listening to the Creation story in Genesis. As newly converted Christians, they were learning to live in a pagan society while still following the ways of Jesus. And how does the greatest missionary and church planter of all time choose to open his letter to the Christians questioning their identity? He alludes to the Mount of Creation story.

3. Read Ephesians 1:3-14 and underline what you learn about redemption and what Christ has done for us.

³ Praise be to the God and Father of our Lord Jesus Christ, who has blessed us in the heavenly realms with every spiritual blessing in Christ. ⁴ For he chose us in him before the creation of the world to be holy and blameless in his sight. In love ⁵ he predestined us for adoption to sonship through Jesus Christ, in accordance with his pleasure and will— ⁶ to the praise of his glorious grace, which he has freely given us in the One he loves. ⁷ In him we have redemption through his blood, the forgiveness of sins, in accordance with the riches of God's grace ⁸ that he lavished on us. With all wisdom and understanding, ⁹ he made known to us the mystery of his will according to his good pleasure, which he purposed in Christ, ¹⁰ to be put into effect when the times reach their fulfillment—to bring unity to all things in heaven and on earth under Christ.

¹¹ In him we were also chosen, having been predestined according to the plan of him who works out everything in conformity with the purpose of his will, ¹² in order that we, who were the first to put our hope in Christ, might be for the praise of his glory. ¹³ And you also were included in Christ when you heard the message of truth, the gospel of your salvation. When you believed, you were marked in him with a seal, the promised Holy Spirit, ¹⁴ who is a deposit guaranteeing our inheritance until the redemption of those who are God's possession—to the praise of his glory.

EPHESIANS 1:3-14

4. As we've discussed before, mountains are biblical images connecting heaven and earth. Now let's connect Mount Eden to Jesus. Reread Ephesians 1:10. How does this passage connect Christ to Eden?

If mountains are where heaven and earth meet, Paul is clarifying that Jesus will eventually remove the divide altogether. Mountains will no longer be the true summit to meet with God because *Jesus is the summit*. Climbing a mountain will no longer be what unites heaven and earth. Jesus will be.

▲　▲　▲

Let's take a look at our storyline.

THE MOUNTAINS STORYLINE OF SCRIPTURE

Location	God's Presence	Revelation
Mount Eden	walking among his people on the mountaintop	God is Creator.
Mount Sinai	descending from the mountaintop with strict parameters	God keeps covenants.
Mount of the Sermon	inviting his disciples to ascend the mountain with him	Jesus fulfills the law.
Mount of Transfiguration	talking with his disciples on top of the mountain	Christ is Messiah.
Mount of the Great Commission	commissioning his disciples to go down from the mountain to go and make disciples	Jesus is with us always.

God's People	Instruction	Identity
Adam and Eve	Do not eat from the Tree of Life.	We are made in God's image, created with purpose and dignity, fashioned to care for God's world and all people.
the Israelites	Obey God's laws.	God's people, the Israelites, the people he rescued and redeemed from slavery, are in a covenant relationship with him that will enable them to be a blessing to all people.
Christ followers	Internalize God's laws.	Christ followers, like the Israelites, are able to internalize God's laws through the power of the Holy Spirit and Christ's example. In doing so, we become a blessing to all people.
Peter, James, and John	Do not be afraid.	Christ followers can stay hopeful through hardship because after the Crucifixion is the Resurrection.
the disciples	Go and make disciples.	Christ followers are commissioned to carry out Jesus' mission but can only do so with Christ's presence.

1. Where in your life do you need the special, concentrated presence of God?

2. What did you learn about God's character in this lesson?

3. How should these truths shape your faith community and change you?

RESPONDING

The purpose of Bible study is to help you become more Christlike; that's why part 4 will include journaling space for your reflection on and responses to the content and a blank checklist for actionable next steps. You'll be able to process what you're learning so that you can live out the concepts and pursue Christlikeness. Part 4 will enable you to answer the questions *What truths is this passage teaching?* and *How do I apply this to my life?*

DO YOU FIND YOURSELF DISORIENTED, not sure where you fit in or what you're supposed to be doing? You're questioning where you belong and who you are meant to be. The Mount Eden story meets you there. Understanding God's heart for us from the very beginning can be a foundational, life-stabilizing force in all of our lives—because a relationship with our Creator secures our identity.

I'm convinced: You and I don't have to waste one more moment feeling uncertain about ourselves. The security you long for can be yours when a covenant relationship with your Creator defines who you are.

The first people to use this Bible study were members of a small group that gathered in my home. As we talked about our questions and insecurities, our group came up with several reasons a secure identity is tied to our origin story in the Garden of Eden.

1. YOUR CREATOR GETS YOU.

Being in relationship with your Creator means that someone truly understands you. Feeling understood is often elusive and fleeting. But who better to "get you" than our Creator? If you need to be known and accepted, turn toward the One who knows you from the inside out. You may feel like a tiny part of God's world, just one piece of the expanse he has created—but I want you to remember that you were designed for this place. Your existence matters to God, enough for him to bring you into his world and entrust you to oversee its care. We need you here.

2. YOUR CREATOR CAN BE TRUSTED.

If God is the Designer, you can trust his plans. If he can speak something into existence from nothing, he can handle the parts of your life that feel overwhelming. When you feel helpless, he is able. The Israelites must have worried that God had forgotten about them or forgotten his promises to them. God's rescue must have seemed so far off, their futures in the palm of their oppressors. But God was working his plan of redemption all along. Old Testament scholar Walter Brueggemann puts it this way: "God can be trusted, even against contemporary data."[13] How do we know for sure? Look around you. His creation speaks of his trustworthiness.

3. YOUR IDENTITY IS TIED TO GOD'S LOVE.

Most of the time, a relationship status or a role or title at work seems to define who we are—but not so for the Christian. Who we are reflects God himself, and God is love. No one and nothing can take away from our relationship with God. Being loved by God is the truest thing about you. You are his.

Use this journaling space to process what you are learning.

Ask yourself how these truths impact your relationship with God and with others.

What is the Holy Spirit bringing to your mind as actionable next steps in your faith journey?

▲

▲

▲

BELIEVING GOD LOVES YOU NO MATTER WHAT

MOUNT SINAI:
WHERE GOD GIVES THE ISRAELITES THE MOSAIC LAW

SCRIPTURE: EXODUS 19–20

PART 1

CONTEXT

Before you begin your study, we will start with the context of the story we are about to read together: the setting, both cultural and historical; the people involved; and where our passage fits in the larger setting of Scripture. All these things help us make sense of what we're reading. Understanding the context of a Bible story is fundamental to reading Scripture well. Getting your bearings before you read will enable you to answer the question *What am I about to read?*

IN AN EPIC LETDOWN, we left Adam and Eve's story in our last lesson as they were exiting the Garden and climbing down the east side of Mount Eden. What began as a holy encounter with their Maker on Mount Eden ended with a journey away from his presence on a trail of uncertainty and fear. Without God near, Adam and Eve were stumbling their way through uncharted territory, assuming they could never turn back.

Had a drone hovered over their downward climb, the footage might have included mournful and tearful emotions heard over the machine's hum. I imagine that their conversations may have included a combination of judgy, deafening silence and blame-filled yelling. I wonder if their self-talk included, *My, how far we've fallen!*

Today, we know that the hope of Mount Eden was not lost, but Adam and Eve didn't know that at the time. And I think their struggle, although very different from our own, is relatable. You and I know what it is to feel cast off and driven out of relationships, jobs, and—for some—a faith community. Living as exiles is lonely and frightening. Even now, you may be struggling with the inevitable feelings that follow being rejected—feeling unloved or unlovable.

Here's the good news: Even when we're living "outside of Eden," we can enjoy God's presence and unfailing love. But how do we get to his presence when he seems far away or we feel rejected?

We don't. He comes to us. And this is really good news. God is always moving toward his people—that's his pattern. We will see God follow this pattern of continually drawing near as he appears to the Israelites at Mount Sinai. God's love for us never fails, and he makes a way to be near us despite us walking away from him the way Adam and Eve walked away from him at Mount Eden.

Like Mount Eden, Mount Sinai represents a place where God's people can enjoy his presence.[1] As Tremper Longman III and Raymond B. Dillard rightly point out, God's presence with the Israelites near Mount Sinai would make it a "holy space and make them a holy people."[2] You can't be in God's orbit without experiencing his holiness and embracing his love. That's why his nearness to us is so important.

While the last lesson focused on a hike down Mount Eden, this lesson zooms in on Moses' ascent of Mount Sinai to receive the Ten Commandments. Now, I know as soon as I mention the Ten Commandments, some of you will be spooked. Stay with me. The words God gave to the Israelites to live by are not punitive, unattainable regulations etched into stone; they are worship-filled, covenant-keeping guidelines for God's chosen people to maintain their loving relationship with God.

Like me, you might view the Old Testament laws with disdain and suspicion. But the truth is that they were a means of God's grace then and they are still helpful to us now. They show us God's heart for his people.

The Israelites approach Mount Sinai as people only recently freed from a nomadic, drama-filled life of slavery under an Egyptian pharaoh. Our God and the Egyptian pharaoh could not be more different. Unlike the Creator, who can make something from nothing, provide everything needed for a flourishing life, and rest when his work is done, the pharaoh was a "hard-nosed production manager for whom production schedules are inexhaustible"[3] who used an exploitative labor system and had punishing expectations, creating "hopeless weariness"[4] in the Israelite slaves.

On Mount Eden, God's image bearers enjoyed the beginnings of a covenant relationship with their Creator. Under Pharaoh's oppression, God's people were no longer celebrated as beloved creatures created by the Creator; they were expendable commodities to be exploited.

Thanks to God, a great exchange happened: Pharaoh for God, slave-commodities for liberated people, and systems of oppression for covenantal love. How? God heard the cries of his weary people and recruited a man named Moses to rescue the slaves through something the Bible calls the Exodus.

I can't emphasize enough the importance of the Exodus. It was the single greatest act of salvation in the Old Testament and became the paradigm for all future deliverances in the Scriptures.[5]

The Exodus story is about how God rescued the Israelites from Pharaoh's tyranny, parting the Red Sea and leading them into the wilderness to worship him freely. Although we usually focus on how God parted the waters of the Red Sea, the prophet Habakkuk retold the story to include God's power over the mountains as well. In Habakkuk 3:6-10, the prophet borrows from the Hebrew imagination and describes the parting of the Red Sea as mountains being shattered and withered and hills sinking low to make way for the torrent of water sweeping over a newly created pathway to freedom.

Make no mistake: God has power over all the mountains in our lives. And if he has to, he will level the peaks we can't climb (Isaiah 40:3-4).

Like a GoPro mounted on a hiking backpack, let's watch together as God

> At Sinai, Israel made a defining choice. It decided to trust the God who made heaven and earth (Exod. 20:11), to rely on the guaranteed reliabilities of the creation, and to eschew the anxiety that comes from loss of confidence in the sureness of the creator and the goodness of creation.[6]
>
> Walter Brueggemann, *Sabbath as Resistance*

brings his newly rescued people back into his presence. In this lesson you're going to read about God giving the law on Mount Sinai—bringing his newly rescued people back into his presence.

My prayer is that you may gain greater confidence in God's love for you, trusting that God loves you *no matter what*. That's the truth. Even if you struggle with confidence in other areas of your life, this is one you can carry with you to the bank: God loves you no matter what.

1. **PERSONAL CONTEXT: What is going on in your life right now that might impact how you understand this Bible story?**

2. **SPIRITUAL CONTEXT: If you've never studied this Bible story before, what piques your curiosity? If you've studied this passage before, what are some things you remember being taught on the subject?**

SEEING

Seeing the text is vital if we want the heart of the Scripture passage to sink in. We read slowly and intentionally through the text with the context in mind. As we practice close, thoughtful reading of Scripture, we pick up on phrases, implications, and meanings we might otherwise have missed. Part 2 includes close Scripture reading and observation questions to empower you to answer the question *What is the story saying?*

1. **Read Exodus 19:1-25 below. As you read,**

   ▲ **underline the words *mountain* and *Sinai*, and**
   ▲ **box the people's response.**

19 On the first day of the third month after the Israelites left Egypt—on that very day—they came to the Desert of Sinai. ² After they set out from Rephidim, they entered the Desert of Sinai, and Israel camped there in the desert in front of the mountain.

   ³ Then Moses went up to God, and the LORD called to him from the mountain and said, "This is what you are to say to the descendants of Jacob and what you are to tell the people of Israel: ⁴ 'You yourselves have seen what I did to Egypt, and how I carried you on eagles' wings and

brought you to myself. [5] Now if you obey me fully and keep my covenant, then out of all nations you will be my treasured possession. Although the whole earth is mine, [6] you will be for me a kingdom of priests and a holy nation.' These are the words you are to speak to the Israelites."

[7] So Moses went back and summoned the elders of the people and set before them all the words the LORD had commanded him to speak. [8] The people all responded together, "We will do everything the LORD has said." So Moses brought their answer back to the LORD.

[9] The LORD said to Moses, "I am going to come to you in a dense cloud, so that the people will hear me speaking with you and will always put their trust in you." Then Moses told the LORD what the people had said.

[10] And the LORD said to Moses, "Go to the people and consecrate them today and tomorrow. Have them wash their clothes [11] and be ready by the third day, because on that day the LORD will come down on Mount Sinai in the sight of all the people. [12] Put limits for the people around the mountain and tell them, 'Be careful that you do not approach the mountain or touch the foot of it. Whoever touches the mountain is to be put to death. [13] They are to be stoned or shot with arrows; not a hand is to be laid on them. No person or animal shall be permitted to live.' Only when the ram's horn sounds a long blast may they approach the mountain."

[14] After Moses had gone down the mountain to the people, he consecrated them, and they washed their clothes. [15] Then he said to the people, "Prepare yourselves for the third day. Abstain from sexual relations."

[16] On the morning of the third day there was thunder and lightning, with a thick cloud over the mountain, and a very loud trumpet blast. Everyone in the camp trembled. [17] Then Moses led the people out of the camp to meet with God, and they stood at the foot of the mountain. [18] Mount Sinai was covered with smoke, because the LORD descended on it in fire. The smoke billowed up from it like smoke from a furnace, and the

whole mountain trembled violently. ¹⁹ As the sound of the trumpet grew louder and louder, Moses spoke and the voice of God answered him.

²⁰ The LORD descended to the top of Mount Sinai and called Moses to the top of the mountain. So Moses went up ²¹ and the LORD said to him, "Go down and warn the people so they do not force their way through to see the LORD and many of them perish. ²² Even the priests, who approach the LORD, must consecrate themselves, or the LORD will break out against them."

²³ Moses said to the LORD, "The people cannot come up Mount Sinai, because you yourself warned us, 'Put limits around the mountain and set it apart as holy.'"

²⁴ The LORD replied, "Go down and bring Aaron up with you. But the priests and the people must not force their way through to come up to the LORD, or he will break out against them."

²⁵ So Moses went down to the people and told them.

EXODUS 19:1-25

2. **Read Exodus 20:1-21 below. As you read, number the Ten Commandments in the margin.**

20 And God spoke all these words:

² "I am the LORD your God, who brought you out of Egypt, out of the land of slavery.

³ "You shall have no other gods before me.

⁴ "You shall not make for yourself an image in the form of anything in heaven above or on the earth beneath or in the waters below. ⁵ You shall not bow down to them or worship them; for I, the LORD your God, am a jealous God, punishing the children for the sin of the parents to the third and fourth generation of those who hate me, ⁶ but showing love to a thousand generations of those who love me and keep my commandments.

⁷ "You shall not misuse the name of the LORD your God, for the LORD will not hold anyone guiltless who misuses his name.

8 "Remember the Sabbath day by keeping it holy. 9 Six days you shall labor and do all your work, 10 but the seventh day is a sabbath to the LORD your God. On it you shall not do any work, neither you, nor your son or daughter, nor your male or female servant, nor your animals, nor any foreigner residing in your towns. 11 For in six days the LORD made the heavens and the earth, the sea, and all that is in them, but he rested on the seventh day. Therefore the LORD blessed the Sabbath day and made it holy.

12 "Honor your father and your mother, so that you may live long in the land the LORD your God is giving you.

13 "You shall not murder.

14 "You shall not commit adultery.

15 "You shall not steal.

16 "You shall not give false testimony against your neighbor.

17 "You shall not covet your neighbor's house. You shall not covet your neighbor's wife, or his male or female servant, his ox or donkey, or anything that belongs to your neighbor."

18 When the people saw the thunder and lightning and heard the trumpet and saw the mountain in smoke, they trembled with fear. They stayed at a distance 19 and said to Moses, "Speak to us yourself and we will listen. But do not have God speak to us or we will die."

20 Moses said to the people, "Do not be afraid. God has come to test you, so that the fear of God will be with you to keep you from sinning."

21 The people remained at a distance, while Moses approached the thick darkness where God was.

EXODUS 20:1-21

> Only as God's law shapes their whole lives will they fulfill their calling and be a blessing to the nations.[7]
>
> Michael W. Goheen and Craig G. Bartholomew, *The True Story of the Whole World*

When God established a covenant relationship between him and his chosen people, they received a "Sinai-given vocation"[8] to be a blessing to all nations.

3. List everything you learn about the Israelites' identity from reading Exodus 19:5-6.

▲

▲

▲

▲

What do the newly liberated Israelites learn about their future? They're going to be set apart to bless everyone. Personally, I'd have a hard time concentrating on my future if I were at the bottom of Mount Sinai. My brain would still be mulling over the drama and horror of generations of oppression in slavery, the plagues in Egypt, and the harrowing journey through the Red Sea.

4. According to Exodus 19:12, what limits did God set concerning Mount Sinai?

The parameters and restrictions God institutes at Sinai are both scary and grace filled—scary because God was serious about his holiness and being obeyed; grace filled because the pathway back to God's presence was being partially restored.

5. Based on Exodus 19:16-19, list all the ways God's presence was revealed.

▲

▲

▲

▲

▲

▲

▲

▲

This combination of natural disasters—a mountain fuming with smoke, earthquake shakes, *and* thunder, *and* lightning—terrifies me. It's a natural wonder the whole lot of them didn't turn around and run away.

6. **Based on Exodus 20:18-21, list all the ways the people responded to God's commands.**

▲

▲

▲

This scene makes a lot of sense to me. The people pushed through their fears and stayed present for the giving of the law, but they kept their distance. Maybe you know the mixed emotions of wanting to be close to God but not wanting to incur his wrath. The Scriptures seem to imply that the people's reaction was acceptable to God since they were not punished. We can be scared and hopeful at the same time.

PART 3

UNDERSTANDING

Now that we've finished a close reading of the Scriptures, we're going to spend some time on interpretation: doing our best to understand what God was saying to the original audience and what he's teaching us through the process. But to do so, we need to learn his ways and consider how God's Word would have been understood by the original audience before applying the same truths to our own lives. "Scripture interpretation" may sound a little stuffy, but understanding what God means to communicate to us in the Bible is crucial to enjoying a close relationship with Jesus. Part 3 will enable you to answer the question *What does it mean?*

UNDERSTANDING MOUNT SINAI

List at least three truths you learned about God in Exodus 19:1–20:21.	How would this truth about God have encouraged the Israelites concerned about God's love?	How does this truth about God build your confidence in God's love?
1.		
2.		
3.		

As the most emblematic example of God's rescuing power, the Exodus story shows up in several other parts of the Bible in summary form. We'll look at just two of those instances:

1. Nehemiah's summary in the Old Testament
2. Stephen's summary in the New Testament

Nehemiah, the great leader who helped rebuild the Jerusalem walls, knew the beginning of the story of redemption well and found his place in it. He believed God would make good on his promises to regather his people in the holy city of Jerusalem and to rebuild the Temple so that God's people could worship freely. He spent his life devoted to rebuilding the ancient ruins of Jerusalem, knowing that God was in the work of restoring all his creation. After the wall around Jerusalem was whole and the exiled Israelites returned and settled, Ezra the priest read the law given at Mount Sinai to all the returned sojourners. To their dismay, they realized they'd not been obeying the law as they should have been—and they responded with national confession and repentance. It's a moving scene. Notice with me how the Mount Sinai story is repurposed in the book of Nehemiah.

1. **Read Nehemiah 9:13-18 and circle everything the Israelites did wrong after receiving the law at Mount Sinai.**

13 "You came down on Mount Sinai; you spoke to them from heaven. You gave them regulations and laws that are just and right, and decrees and commands that are good. 14 You made known to them your holy Sabbath and gave them commands, decrees and laws through your servant Moses.

¹⁵ In their hunger you gave them bread from heaven and in their thirst you brought them water from the rock; you told them to go in and take possession of the land you had sworn with uplifted hand to give them.

¹⁶ "But they, our ancestors, became arrogant and stiff-necked, and they did not obey your commands. ¹⁷ They refused to listen and failed to remember the miracles you performed among them. They became stiff-necked and in their rebellion appointed a leader in order to return to their slavery. But you are a forgiving God, gracious and compassionate, slow to anger and abounding in love. Therefore you did not desert them, ¹⁸ even when they cast for themselves an image of a calf and said, 'This is your god, who brought you up out of Egypt,' or when they committed awful blasphemies."

NEHEMIAH 9:13-18

2. **How would you describe the Israelites' post-Sinai behavior (see Nehemiah 9:16-17)?**

3. **In Nehemiah 9:17, what do you learn about God's character?**

1.

2.

3.

4.

Just when we start to think God's people, the Israelites, will break the cycle of rebellion begun on Mount Eden, we are disappointed by their disobedience to the law given at Mount Sinai. But we also understand it, don't we? We all know how tempting and easy it is to slide back into an unhealthy or sinful pattern. Like us, the Israelites disobeyed God. But thankfully, God's love doesn't depend on us being obedient. God's love is never removed from our lives because he can't change his character; God is love, and he always will be.

Now, let's connect God's encounter with his people at Mount Sinai to Jesus in the New Testament. One of Jesus' followers was a man named Stephen. Stephen was best known for speaking truth to power with grace, performing signs and wonders in the synagogue, and preaching Jesus as Messiah. This put him in hot water with Jewish religious leaders and even with the high priest. When a council of religious elite questioned him, Stephen responded with a sermon that schooled the Jewish priests on how Jesus fulfilled the Torah. Enraged by his sermon, they stoned Stephen to death.

What was so controversial about Stephen's last sermon? See for yourself.

4. **Read Acts 7:17-39, circling every time Moses is mentioned.**

[17] "As the time drew near for the fulfillment of the promise that God had made to Abraham, our people in Egypt increased and multiplied [18] until another king who had not known Joseph ruled over Egypt. [19] He dealt craftily with our race and forced our ancestors to abandon their infants so that they would die. [20] At this time Moses was born, and he was beautiful before God. For three months he was brought up in his father's house; [21] and when he was abandoned, Pharaoh's daughter adopted him and brought him up as her own son. [22] So Moses was

instructed in all the wisdom of the Egyptians and was powerful in his words and deeds.

[23] "When he was forty years old, it came into his heart to visit his relatives, the Israelites. [24] When he saw one of them being wronged, he defended the oppressed man and avenged him by striking down the Egyptian. [25] He supposed that his kinsfolk would understand that God through him was rescuing them, but they did not understand. [26] The next day he came to some of them as they were quarreling and tried to reconcile them, saying, 'Men, you are brothers; why do you wrong each other?' [27] But the man who was wronging his neighbor pushed Moses aside, saying, 'Who made you a ruler and a judge over us? [28] Do you want to kill me as you killed the Egyptian yesterday?' [29] When he heard this, Moses fled and became a resident alien in the land of Midian. There he became the father of two sons.

[30] "Now when forty years had passed, an angel appeared to him in the wilderness of Mount Sinai, in the flame of a burning bush. [31] When Moses saw it, he was amazed at the sight; and as he approached to look, there came the voice of the Lord: [32] 'I am the God of your ancestors, the God of Abraham, Isaac, and Jacob.' Moses began to tremble and did not dare to look. [33] Then the Lord said to him, 'Take off the sandals from your feet, for the place where you are standing is holy ground. [34] I have surely seen the mistreatment of my people who are in Egypt and have heard their groaning, and I have come down to rescue them. Come now, I will send you to Egypt.'

[35] "It was this Moses whom they rejected when they said, 'Who made you a ruler and a judge?' and whom God now sent as both ruler and liberator through the angel who appeared to him in the bush. [36] He led them out, having performed wonders and signs in Egypt, at the Red Sea, and in the wilderness for forty years. [37] This is the Moses who said to the Israelites, 'God will raise up a prophet for you from your own people as he raised me up.' [38] He is the one who was in the congregation in the

wilderness with the angel who spoke to him at Mount Sinai, and with our ancestors; and he received living oracles to give to us. ³⁹ Our ancestors were unwilling to obey him; instead, they pushed him aside, and in their hearts they turned back to Egypt."

ACTS 7:17-39, NRSV

Doesn't Stephen's sermon sound familiar? It is very similar to Ezra's sermon.

The reason Stephen's sermon sent the Jerusalem council over the edge was the suggestion that they were like their ancestors, refusing to obey God and rejecting Christ in their hearts. Stephen must have been an Enneagram Eight, the protector, issuing this bold challenge. Here's the conclusion to Stephen's sermon before he was stoned to death.

5. Read Act 7:51-53, circling every time the word _you_ appears.

⁵¹ "You stiff-necked people, uncircumcised in heart and ears, you are forever opposing the Holy Spirit, just as your ancestors used to do. ⁵² Which of the prophets did your ancestors not persecute? They killed those who foretold the coming of the Righteous One, and now you have become his betrayers and murderers. ⁵³ You are the ones that received the law as ordained by angels, and yet you have not kept it."

ACTS 7:51-53, NRSV

This much shade from Stephen makes me chuckle a little. I can imagine the crowd slack-jawed and offended. But his sermon also convicts me—deeply. I know I'm not living a completely righteous life; none of us can. We are in this together.

In our next lesson, we'll focus our time on practical ways to let God's laws change us. Until then, we need to receive the Mount Sinai story with some balance, equal parts conviction and encouragement. No, God's laws are not yet perfected in our lives—but he is making a way. He is moving to change us with the same power he used to lead the people of Israel out of Egypt, through the Red Sea, and up close to him on Mount Sinai.

▲　▲　▲

Let's check back in on our Mountains Storyline.

THE MOUNTAINS STORYLINE OF SCRIPTURE

Location	God's Presence	Revelation
Mount Eden	walking among his people on the mountaintop	God is Creator.
Mount Sinai	descending from the mountaintop with strict parameters	God keeps covenants.
Mount of the Sermon	inviting his disciples to ascend the mountain with him	Jesus fulfills the law.
Mount of Transfiguration	talking with his disciples on top of the mountain	Christ is Messiah.
Mount of the Great Commission	commissioning his disciples to go down from the mountain to go and make disciples	Jesus is with us always.

God's People	Instruction	Identity
Adam and Eve	Do not eat from the Tree of Life.	We are made in God's image, created with purpose and dignity, fashioned to care for God's world and all people.
the Israelites	Obey God's laws.	God's people, the Israelites, the people he rescued and redeemed from slavery, are in a covenant relationship with him that will enable them to bea blessing to all people.
Christ followers	Internalize God's laws.	Christ followers, like the Israelites, are able to internalize God's laws through the power of the Holy Spirit and Christ's example. In doing so, we become a blessing to all people.
Peter, James, and John	Do not be afraid.	Christ followers can stay hopeful through hardship because after the Crucifixion is the Resurrection.
the disciples	Go and make disciples.	Christ followers are commissioned to carry out Jesus' mission but can only do so with Christ's presence.

1. Where in your life do you need the special, concentrated presence of God?

2. What did you learn about God's character in this lesson?

3. How should these truths shape your faith community and change you?

RESPONDING

The purpose of Bible study is to help you become more Christlike; that's why part 4 will include journaling space for your reflection on and responses to the content and a blank checklist for actionable next steps. You'll be able to process what you're learning so that you can live out the concepts and pursue Christlikeness. Part 4 will enable you to answer the questions *What truths is this passage teaching?* and *How do I apply this to my life?*

MY SON, CALEB, loved his second-grade teacher, Mrs. Hyde. Mrs. Hyde is a hero simply because she is an educator, but she rose to fame in our home while leading class online during pandemic quarantine. I had the privilege of overhearing Mrs. Hyde tell her class that she loved them via Zoom and held back tears until my throat ached.

When I asked Caleb to describe Mrs. Hyde, he said she was "strict and loving." I think Caleb's statement could describe God, too. He is strict in that he expects us to obey his laws and his ways. And he is loving in that he cares about us regardless of whether we live up to his expectations.

Even if you feel like you've blown it, here are a few reasons you can be confident in God's love for you.

1. GOD'S LOVE CAME BEFORE HIS LAW WAS GIVEN.

I'm overjoyed that the Exodus happened before the giving of the law. The paradigmatic act of God's salvation for his people, the proof of his love—the Exodus—came *before* he showed them how to live out his creational intentions in the law.

You see, in God's story, from Genesis to Revelation, he rescues us before keeping us accountable to his ways. This is good news. I'm more aware of my sinfulness now than I was even a few weeks ago. With each turning of the calendar year, I recognize in fuller measure just how much I need Jesus. But even as my awareness grows, the reality of his rescue doesn't change: I stand solid, knowing he continues to move toward me, that the path to relationship is not dependent on my performance but on his salvation. I can continue to move into Christlikeness with the confidence of a loved child whose status will not change based on mistakes. Attempting to live by his standards before experiencing his saving grace is not the way of Jesus. Grace before law, always. You can be confident in God's love because he loved you long before you knew what was right and wrong.

2. GOD'S LOVE IS NOT CONDITIONAL OR BASED ON OBEDIENCE TO THE LAW.

We might need a perspective shift when it comes to the Ten Commandments. As Old Testament professor Carmen Imes says in her book *Bearing God's Name: Why Sinai Still Matters,*

> The law was never the means by which Israel earned God's favor. The Israelites were saved the same way we are—by grace through faith. But their obedience expressed their covenant commitment, or allegiance, to Yahweh. And it kept them in a position to experience the benefits of the covenant relationship.[10]

God anticipated the Israelites' disobedience to the law and kept making a way to be in a loving relationship with them. You can be confident in God's love for you because his love is not conditional.

3. GOD'S LOVE CAN BE TRUSTED.

God's people were receptive to the Ten Commandments because they were a people formed through a great act of redemption. Not one of them could deny or forget just how close they had come to death in their escape from Egypt—and just how mightily the Lord would act to ensure their safety. Their God could be trusted. Trusted to listen to their pain and suffering. Trusted to move mountains and make a way of escape. Trusted to deliver them from oppression. And trusted to make promises only the one true, living God could keep. You, too, can be confident in God's love.

4. CONFIDENCE IN GOD'S LOVE TAKES PRACTICE.

One aspect of the Mount Sinai story in particular grabs my attention: the fire. No wonder the people of God were scared to approach the mountain—it was up in flames. I'm convinced one of the reasons Moses handled the giving of the law with less trepidation than the people was because he had seen God in the burning bush on Mount Sinai months earlier. This was not his first time near the open flames of God Almighty. Moses likely assumed that Mount Sinai would not be consumed because the burning bush surely hadn't been. But to the wilderness-weary ex-slaves, I wonder if all they could see was a whole mountain ablaze. Moses was less scared to receive God's love at Mount Sinai because he had more practice accepting God's love and holiness. If you are resisting and doubting God's love for you, be gentle with yourself. Just as becoming a loving person takes practice, becoming a loved person takes practice too.

> The Israelites' delivery from bondage was not conditional on their keeping the law, and keeping or not keeping the law was not going to hasten or delay their deliverance. No, the Lord acted first. He took the initiative and redeemed his people from the bondage of slavery and made a covenant with them. Keeping his law was to be an act of gratitude in response to what the Lord had done.[11]
>
> P. G. George and Paul Swarup, "Exodus," in *South Asia Bible Commentary*

▲ ▲ ▲

Although we don't see the whole nation climbing back up Sinai to restore what Adam and Eve lost on Mount Eden, we do see God nearer to his people at Mount Sinai. What we will see in the next lesson is Jesus coming as a new and better Moses to bring God's people closer to God. And he does it through a famous sermon on—you guessed it—a mountain.

Use this journaling space to process what you are learning.

Ask yourself how these truths impact your relationship with God and with others.

What is the Holy Spirit bringing to your mind as actionable next steps in your faith journey?

▲

▲

▲

RECONSTRUCTING YOUR FAITH IN AN AGE OF DECONSTRUCTION

MOUNT OF THE SERMON:
WHERE JESUS DELIVERS HIS MOST FAMOUS MESSAGE

SCRIPTURE: MATTHEW 5

PART 1

CONTEXT

Before you begin your study, we will start with the context of the story we are about to read together: the setting, both cultural and historical; the people involved; and where our passage fits in the larger setting of Scripture. All these things help us make sense of what we're reading. Understanding the context of a Bible story is fundamental to reading Scripture well. Getting your bearings before you read will enable you to answer the question *What am I about to read?*

EVERYWHERE I TURN THESE DAYS, I'm invited into conversations with disillusioned Christians leaving the church. Some are not just detaching from a local church or a particular Christian institution; they are throwing the peace sign and walking away from their faith altogether. These men and women confiding in me are suffering through an erosion of trust—in the faith of their youth and in fallen leaders. As credibility crumbles, hurting people are deconstructing what used to anchor them to Jesus.

It's not lost on me that you might feel as if I've been reading your mail. Maybe you're out of church but all-in for Jesus; disconnected from organized religion but clinging to the Jesus of the gospel. Church hurt didn't just add a limp to your faith walk—you feel sidelined from a faith community, and you're not sure you ever want to go back. If church hurt is your story, there's plenty of space in this study for Jesus to tenderly bind up your injuries. You are safe in his tender care. This lesson is for anyone nursing pain points like judgmental, hypocritical Christians; fallen faith leaders; or ministry conflict.

Yes, our faith leaders have always been imperfect—and the church today is in the middle of a great revealing. Yet I remain hopeful because the uncovering of sin could lead to a great wave of repentance and reformation.

Thankfully, we are not alone in this reckoning. Through the centuries, our brothers and sisters in the faith have challenged the status quo many times over. In some cases, the people of God have chosen to repent and rebuild. We will see an example of that in our mountaintop story from Matthew 5.

We will also see that purposing to *do* better won't cut it. We have to *become* the kind of people who are able to do better. How do we do that? Every decaying and rotten plank in our spiritual house needs gutting. We must live repentantly and in a constant state of rebuilding our faith based on what we learn from Christ.

As Christ followers, Christlikeness is our goal. We need Jesus to transform our character so that it increasingly looks like his own. And not because saving the church is our responsibility—God needs no help from us to salvage the remnant; nothing threatens the church—but because Christianity is about becoming like Jesus.

The way of Jesus must become our firm foundation. And the sturdy, weight-bearing beams of Kingdom ethics have to frame out our faith for reconstruction. Dallas Willard said it better and maybe more clearly: "It is the inner life of the soul that we must aim to transform."[1]

This week you'll see what it looks like when God's demo day is followed up with heart renovations. More specifically, what it looks like when the Torah—the law given to God's people at Mount Sinai—is not just obeyed but also reconstructs who we are to our core, shaping our inner, spiritual lives with Kingdom values. The law was designed not just to differentiate good behavior from bad but to present a way of living that subverts "the entire edifice of human corruption."[2]

In short, the law of God, rooted in our hearts, looks like Jesus. And Jesus will call us to follow him so closely that our own lives will embody the spirit of the law. The laws Jesus presents to us through his Sermon on the Mount in Matthew 5–7 are not etched onto stone tablets as on Mount Sinai; they are ingrained in our hearts through Christ's love and the power of the Holy Spirit.

Jesus came as a new Moses on a new mountain to *fulfill* the laws of God in his Sermon on the Mount.

Before we read part of Jesus' most famous sermon, notice with me the harmony between the mountain settings God used as a backdrop for the giving of the law at Mount Sinai *and* Jesus' fulfilling of the law in the Sermon on the Mount. First, let's look at the overlap between the arbiters of the law in both mountaintop stories: Moses and Jesus. I don't want you to miss that the Gospel writer, Matthew, "is clearly writing within the stream of the Jewish tradition, and this comes out in these verses with his implicit figural connection between Jesus and Moses."[3] Jonathan Pennington's theological commentary on Jesus' famous message, *The Sermon on the Mount and Human Flourishing*, helped me pull together this table that I hope will give you a visual of the Moses-Jesus motif we're going to study together.[4]

HARMONY BETWEEN MOSES AND JESUS

	Moses	Jesus
As infants, both were miraculously spared from a ruler's order to slaughter children.	Exodus 1–2	Matthew 2
Both left the land and returned at God's direction.	Exodus 2–4	Matthew 2
Both experienced a temptation in the wilderness.	Exodus 15:22-25	Matthew 4
Both spent forty days and nights fasting on a mount of revelation.	Exodus 34	Matthew 4
Both passed through water.	Exodus 14	Matthew 3
Both delivered the law from a mountain.	Exodus 19–20	Matthew 5-7
Both are arbiters of God's law.	Exodus 19–20	Matthew 5-7
Both are rescuers: Moses helped rescue God's people through the Exodus. Jesus, the Messiah, leads us to salvation and an exodus from sin.	Exodus 14	Matthew 27-28

MOUNTAINTOP EXPERIENCES IN MATTHEW

I recently made a road trip to College Station, Texas, after not visiting for several years. Despite so much of Aggieland looking different, twenty years after my college graduation, the whole city was a walk down memory lane. Every corner was a reminder of treasured experiences in that college town. A look to my left, and I caught a glimpse of the coffee shop I used to stake out at in hopes of running into my now-husband, Aaron. A drive past the football stadium, and next thing I know, I'm misty-eyed, seeing the press box where Aaron proposed. Honestly, it doesn't matter what street I am on in College Station or the purpose for the visit; the place represents falling in love with my husband.

In the same way that College Station brings up meaningful memories in my life, Matthew's Gospel highlights several mountainsides to remind his audience of the rich heritage of revelatory mountain scenes in Israel's history. Several times while preparing this Bible study, I referenced one of Ian Boxall's commentaries on Matthew, where he summarizes how these high places are powerful theological symbols of God meeting with his people:

> Particular places contain a complex web of association and memory, linked to what has occurred there or people who have been there in the past, which may be triggered by the mere mention of their name.[5]

Boxall is quick to point out that reading the book of Matthew correctly means appreciating the mountain settings in the stories as carriers of symbolic function and preservers of memories.[6] Terence Donaldson, in his book *Jesus on the Mountain*, says something similar: "Matthew intended for mountains to not just be a literary device but also a theological symbol."[7]

Holy mountains can have the same prominent role in your life as they do in the Bible. The stories we read in this study can be a place where God meets you in the same way they served as settings for revelation and divine encounters with God for the Israelites. And maybe that's just what you need—an encounter with God. Something that reminds you he is real, he cares, and he's close.

Inspired by professor of New Testament and Jewish studies Amy-Jill Levine's mad summarization skills in her book *The Sermon on the Mount: A Beginner's Guide to the Kingdom of Heaven*, I've pulled together an overview of some of the memorable mountain moments in Matthew's Gospel.[8] (Try saying that three times fast.)

MOUNTAINS IN MATTHEW

Matthew 4	**Jesus' testing on a mountain.** Right after Jesus is baptized, he enters the wilderness for forty days and nights to be tested. During the encounter, the enemy takes him to a mountain to be tested.
Matthew 5–7	**The Sermon on the Mount.** This is Jesus' most famous sermon, and portions of it are quoted by other Gospel writers.
Matthew 15	**The feeding of the four thousand.** Jesus performed many feeding miracles where he fed large crowds of people, usually numbering in the thousands. He had the power to multiply measly portions of food into an abundance of servings to meet the needs of the hungry people on a mountain.
Matthew 17	**The Transfiguration.** We'll study this in the next lesson. Jesus brings Peter, James, and John up a mountain, being transformed in front of their eyes as he is joined by Moses and Elijah.
Matthew 24–25	**The Olivet Discourse.** While preaching his last set of sermons on the Mount of Olives, Jesus teaches about the future of the church.
Matthew 28	**The Great Commission.** We'll study this in the last lesson. Jesus gathers his disciples to commission them to share God's love with all.

Our relational, covenant-keeping God is about to show off his love and grace as he reveals what wholehearted devotion could look like in your life and mine. Spoiler alert: When our heart condition aligns with the spirit of God's laws, we become more Christlike.

1. **PERSONAL CONTEXT: What is going on in your life right now that might impact how you understand this Bible story?**

2. **SPIRITUAL CONTEXT: If you've never studied this Bible story before, what piques your curiosity? If you've studied this passage before, what are some things you remember being taught on the subject?**

SEEING

Seeing the text is vital if we want the heart of the Scripture passage to sink in. We read slowly and intentionally through the text with the context in mind. As we practice close, thoughtful reading of Scripture, we pick up on phrases, implications, and meanings we might otherwise have missed. Part 2 includes close Scripture reading and observation questions to empower you to answer the question *What is the story saying?*

1. **Read Matthew 4:23–5:16 below. As you read, underline the various kinds of people following Jesus up the mountainside.**

²³ Jesus went throughout Galilee, teaching in their synagogues, proclaiming the good news of the kingdom, and healing every disease and sickness among the people. ²⁴ News about him spread all over Syria, and people brought to him all who were ill with various diseases, those suffering severe pain, the demon-possessed, those having seizures, and the paralyzed; and he healed them. ²⁵ Large crowds from Galilee, the Decapolis, Jerusalem, Judea and the region across the Jordan followed him.

5 Now when Jesus saw the crowds, he went up on a mountainside and sat down. His disciples came to him, ² and he began to teach them.

He said:

3 "Blessed are the poor in spirit,
   for theirs is the kingdom of heaven.
4 Blessed are those who mourn,
   for they will be comforted.
5 Blessed are the meek,
   for they will inherit the earth.
6 Blessed are those who hunger and thirst for righteousness,
   for they will be filled.
7 Blessed are the merciful,
   for they will be shown mercy.
8 Blessed are the pure in heart,
   for they will see God.
9 Blessed are the peacemakers,
   for they will be called children of God.
10 Blessed are those who are persecuted because of righteousness,
   for theirs is the kingdom of heaven.

11 "Blessed are you when people insult you, persecute you and falsely say all kinds of evil against you because of me. 12 Rejoice and be glad, because great is your reward in heaven, for in the same way they persecuted the prophets who were before you.

13 "You are the salt of the earth. But if the salt loses its saltiness, how can it be made salty again? It is no longer good for anything, except to be thrown out and trampled underfoot.

14 "You are the light of the world. A town built on a hill cannot be hidden. 15 Neither do people light a lamp and put it under a bowl. Instead they put it on its stand, and it gives light to everyone in the house. 16 In the same way, let your light shine before others, that they may see your good deeds and glorify your Father in heaven."

MATTHEW 4:23–5:16

2. **Read Matthew 5:17–48 below. As you read, keep count of each time you see a phrase similar to "you have heard that it was said" by numbering or tallying in the margin.**

[17] "Do not think that I have come to abolish the Law or the Prophets; I have not come to abolish them but to fulfill them. [18] For truly I tell you, until heaven and earth disappear, not the smallest letter, not the least stroke of a pen, will by any means disappear from the Law until everything is accomplished. [19] Therefore anyone who sets aside one of the least of these commands and teaches others accordingly will be called least in the kingdom of heaven, but whoever practices and teaches these commands will be called great in the kingdom of heaven. [20] For I tell you that unless your righteousness surpasses that of the Pharisees and the teachers of the law, you will certainly not enter the kingdom of heaven.

[21] "You have heard that it was said to the people long ago, 'You shall not murder, and anyone who murders will be subject to judgment.' [22] But I tell you that anyone who is angry with a brother or sister will be subject to judgment. Again, anyone who says to a brother or sister, 'Raca,' is answerable to the court. And anyone who says, 'You fool!' will be in danger of the fire of hell.

[23] "Therefore, if you are offering your gift at the altar and there remember that your brother or sister has something against you, [24] leave your gift there in front of the altar. First go and be reconciled to them; then come and offer your gift.

[25] "Settle matters quickly with your adversary who is taking you to court. Do it while you are still together on the way, or your adversary may hand you over to the judge, and the judge may hand you over to the officer, and you may be thrown into prison. [26] Truly I tell you, you will not get out until you have paid the last penny.

[27] "You have heard that it was said, 'You shall not commit adultery.' [28] But I tell you that anyone who looks at a woman lustfully has already committed adultery with her in his heart. [29] If your right eye causes you to stumble, gouge it out and throw it away. It is better for you to lose one

part of your body than for your whole body to be thrown into hell. [30] And if your right hand causes you to stumble, cut it off and throw it away. It is better for you to lose one part of your body than for your whole body to go into hell.

[31] "It has been said, 'Anyone who divorces his wife must give her a certificate of divorce.' [32] But I tell you that anyone who divorces his wife, except for sexual immorality, makes her the victim of adultery, and anyone who marries a divorced woman commits adultery.

[33] "Again, you have heard that it was said to the people long ago, 'Do not break your oath, but fulfill to the Lord the vows you have made.' [34] But I tell you, do not swear an oath at all: either by heaven, for it is God's throne; [35] or by the earth, for it is his footstool; or by Jerusalem, for it is the city of the Great King. [36] And do not swear by your head, for you cannot make even one hair white or black. [37] All you need to say is simply 'Yes' or 'No'; anything beyond this comes from the evil one.

[38] "You have heard that it was said, 'Eye for eye, and tooth for tooth.' [39] But I tell you, do not resist an evil person. If anyone slaps you on the right cheek, turn to them the other cheek also. [40] And if anyone wants to sue you and take your shirt, hand over your coat as well. [41] If anyone forces you to go one mile, go with them two miles. [42] Give to the one who asks you, and do not turn away from the one who wants to borrow from you.

[43] "You have heard that it was said, 'Love your neighbor and hate your enemy.' [44] But I tell you, love your enemies and pray for those who persecute you, [45] that you may be children of your Father in heaven. He causes his sun to rise on the evil and the good, and sends rain on the righteous and the unrighteous. [46] If you love those who love you, what reward will you get? Are not even the tax collectors doing that? [47] And if you greet only your own people, what are you doing more than others? Do not even pagans do that? [48] Be perfect, therefore, as your heavenly Father is perfect."

MATTHEW 5:17-48

> *A quick note to abuse survivors*: If the church has demonized you for divorcing an abusive partner and used Jesus' words in the Sermon on the Mount to shame, condemn, or judge you, that's wrong. If you are in an abusive relationship, your safety is Jesus' priority. You can call this number if you need help: 1-800-799-7233.

3. **Take time to fill out the second column to help you carefully process what Jesus is saying (and not saying).**

HOW JESUS FUFILLS THE TORAH

Torah: "You have heard it said . . ."	Jesus: "But I tell you . . ."
Do not murder.	1. (Matthew 5:22)
Do not commit adultery.	2. (Matthew 5:28)
Use certificates of divorce.	3. (Matthew 5:32)
Don't break oaths.	4. (Matthew 5:34)

Take an eye for an eye.	5. (Matthew 5:39)
Love your neighbor.	6. (Matthew 5:44)

You might be tempted, like I was, to think of Christ's words as a replacement for the law God gave on Mount Sinai—an out-with-the-old, in-with-the-new situation. Instead, I want you to consider Jesus' own words as our directions for interpretation.

4. Write out what Jesus says in Matthew 5:17.

Jesus was not destroying the law or undermining it; he was *fulfilling* it. (We will explore this more soon.) As Jesus was consummating the purpose of the law and renovating hearts, he was also inaugurating a new era with a new covenant, just as the prophet Jeremiah had predicted ages before.[9] The prophet Jeremiah would receive messages from God and share them with God's people. In one portion of the book of Jeremiah in the Old Testament, Jeremiah talks about the reconstruction of our faith under Jesus' new covenant. He doesn't use Jesus' name, but we now know that that's exactly what he was predicting. I want you to take a second and write out a few of Jeremiah's words of comfort to a people sick and tired of disappointing God and being disappointed in God's people.

5. Write out Jeremiah 31:31-33 below:

We need more than inscriptions telling us what to do (and not do); we need the Holy Spirit's will to help us choose obedience. We need our hearts changed by God's love so that we can do what's right.

PART 3

UNDERSTANDING

Now that we've finished a close reading of the Scriptures, we're going to spend some time on interpretation: doing our best to understand what God was saying to the original audience and what he's teaching us through the process. But to do so, we need to learn his ways and consider how God's Word would have been understood by the original audience before applying the same truths to our own lives. "Scripture interpretation" may sound a little stuffy, but understanding what God means to communicate to us in the Bible is crucial to enjoying a close relationship with Jesus. Part 3 will enable you to answer the question *What does it mean?*

YOU CAN KNOW THE RIGHT THING TO DO and the right way to live and still resist letting that truth travel from your head to your heart. This is my story. Maybe it's yours, too. If we're honest, we all find ourselves in that place more often than we'd like. I know right from wrong, but sometimes I willingly choose to sin—after a whole lot of back-and-forth that happens in my heart. I bargain with myself, justify the potential outcomes, and ask my conscience to hush.

If we are building our faith back up, brick by brick, we need to pay careful attention to Jesus' Sermon on the Mount message. Although his sermon is long, it has one main point: To truly honor God, we need the spirit of God's laws embedded in the interior of our being.

If I were to summarize each of the six laws Jesus brings up in his Sermon on the Mount, I would condense his message this way:

1. Murder starts in your heart.
2. Adultery starts in your heart.
3. Divorce starts in your heart.
4. Oath breaking starts in your heart.
5. Retaliation starts in your heart.
6. Love for your enemy starts in your heart.

1. **Review the list above and write out which of Jesus' laws jumps out to you the most and why.**

2. **How do you see this truth playing out in your own life?**

Jesus was not abolishing the law; he was deconstructing how we apply his teaching and reconstructing our applications—to show us what kind of people can keep the law. I find myself squirming with conviction when I read the summary list above. When I want to "become a better person," I often focus on trying harder, doing more, or saying less. Rarely does my remedy ever work. In fact, more often than not, I end up more frustrated that my efforts fail. The beauty of the Jesus way is that allowing his laws into our heart of hearts changes us from the inside out.

MAKING CONNECTIONS

An important part of understanding the meaning of a Bible passage is getting a sense of its place in the broader storyline of Scripture. When we make connections between different parts of the Bible, we get a glimpse of the unity and cohesion of the Scriptures.

Before applying what we've been learning in this lesson to our everyday lives, let's review some of the patterns emerging in our study of mountaintop experiences in the Bible. I want you to see the beautiful tapestry God is weaving with these stories set on or near mountains. We've looked at Mount Eden, Mount Sinai, and now the Sermon on the Mount. All three stories share not only a mountain backdrop but also several key elements:

- ▲ the special, concentrated presence of God;
- ▲ a history-changing revelation of God's character;
- ▲ the forming of a faith community or a people of faith; and
- ▲ important teaching or instructions from God about how to live his way.

These stand-out elements bring together a cohesive storyline:

THE MOUNTAINS STORYLINE OF SCRIPTURE

Location	God's Presence	Revelation
Mount Eden	walking among his people on the mountaintop	God is Creator.
Mount Sinai	descending from the mountaintop with strict parameters	God keeps covenants.
Mount of the Sermon	inviting his disciples to ascend the mountain with him	Jesus fulfills the law.
Mount of Transfiguration	talking with his disciples on top of the mountain	Christ is Messiah.
Mount of the Great Commission	commissioning his disciples to go down from the mountain to go and make disciples	Jesus is with us always.

God's People	Instruction	Identity
Adam and Eve	Do not eat from the Tree of Life.	We are made in God's image, created with purpose and dignity, fashioned to care for God's world and all people.
the Israelites	Obey God's laws.	God's people, the Israelites, the people he rescued and redeemed from slavery, are in a covenant relationship with him that will enable them to bea blessing to all people.
Christ followers	Internalize God's laws.	Christ followers, like the Israelites, are able to internalize God's laws through the power of the Holy Spirit and Christ's example. In doing so, we become a blessing to all people.
Peter, James, and John	Do not be afraid.	Christ followers can stay hopeful through hardship because after the Crucifixion is the Resurrection.
the disciples	Go and make disciples.	Christ followers are commissioned to carry out Jesus' mission but can only do so with Christ's presence.

1. **Where in your life do you need the special, concentrated presence of God?**

2. **What did you learn about God's character in this lesson?**

3. **How should these truths shape your faith community and change you?**

RESPONDING

The purpose of Bible study is to help you become more Christlike; that's why part 4 will include journaling space for your reflection on and responses to the content and a blank checklist for actionable next steps. You'll be able to process what you're learning so that you can live out the concepts and pursue Christlikeness. Part 4 will enable you to answer the questions *What truths is this passage teaching?* and *How do I apply this to my life?*

BEFORE MY FATHER PASSED AWAY, he remodeled homes for a living. I think construction was his first and true love, as far as work was concerned. He did everything from flipping homes to becoming a real estate agent to overseeing construction builds. Part of the reason I dedicated this study to him was because I think he would have loved having a conversation with me about the crucial elements of reconstruction once demolition is done on a home. He loved remodels, and he loved Jesus.

My dad was an especially tenderhearted person with compassion for anyone struggling to trust Christians. He probably didn't know the term "church hurt," but he was practiced in sitting with someone marginalized as an outsider.

It's times like these I miss my dad the most. I wish I could pick up the phone and ask him some quick questions about the illustration I want to share with you. Instead, I reached out to my friend Mike, who owns a construction company. I'm certain my dad and Mike would have been fast friends.

The smell of fresh paint filled up my nose as Mike and I did a walk-through of one of his projects just days before his clients moved in. I marveled at the transformation process, noting all the finishes I loved—kitchen pulls, lighting fixtures, and especially the bathroom tile. Goodness, the bathroom tile. I joke with my husband, Aaron, that if for some reason I was taken hostage in our bathroom, I'd rather accept my fate than let the police—anyone, really—into our bathroom. It needs a total overhaul.

As I stood in Mike's latest masterpiece, awing over the bathroom makeover, Mike commented that the project was a success because the owner knew exactly how they wanted the home to look before they even started demolition. It wasn't enough, Mike said, for the owners of the house to want a beautiful, new interior as the final product; they had to have the end in mind precisely—all the decisions about how many faucets and what kind determined positioning, installation, plumbing, and wiring. Which got me thinking about how we can apply Jesus' Sermon on the Mount to our lives.

1. BLUEPRINT YOUR RECONSTRUCTION PLAN.

Jesus' Sermon on the Mount is not just about demolition to the rotten parts of our faith—it's about renovating our hearts to live out the law. His sermon serves as our blueprint for reconstructing our faith with the end in mind. I wonder if some of us have hailed a bulldozer to our spiritual houses with every intention of a faith remodel but instead gotten stuck with all the debris gutted in demolition. Maybe we started demolition before the blueprint was finalized. It would be just like me to think I could figure out the finishes near the end of the remodel only to realize that mid-project is not the right time to call the plumber back out to move a pipe.

2. ANTICIPATE REBUILDING DELAYS AND UNEXPECTED COSTS.

Every time Aaron and I have made construction changes to our home, we've grossly underestimated the cost and time of the project. It is the same when we are building up our faith after we've spent an extended time in rubble. Any number of distractions and setbacks might tempt us to give up all together. Perhaps that's one of the reasons why Jesus tells us to count the cost (Luke 14:28). Rebuilding after desolation is heavy and hard. We'll discover other places that feel shaky. We'll face obstacles and endure delays. But when we set our expectations rightly—that strengthening our faith and reconstructing toward what is true will cost us more than we want to give and take longer than we hope—we will make it through. And I can assure you of this: It will be worth it.

Before you give up on the reconstruction, before you give up on the church, I want to encourage you—you are not left alone and abandoned. Jesus is an expert renovator with a foolproof blueprint. You might not be able to trust Christians, the church, or even yourself in this renovation process, but you can trust Jesus. You can build your faith on him. Jesus can be your foundation. Jesus can be your load-bearing beams. *He* can be your blueprint. Maybe your first step is to welcome the Sermon on the Mount into your heart and trust God's master trade skills. When Jesus is the foundation of your faith, you're rebuilding on a firm foundation.

Use this journaling space to process what you are learning.

Ask yourself how these truths impact your relationship with God and with others.

What is the Holy Spirit bringing to your mind as actionable next steps in your faith journey?

▲

▲

▲

GROWING HOPEFUL
WHEN YOUR LIFE IS HARD

MOUNT OF TRANSFIGURATION:
WHERE JESUS REVEALS HIS GLORY TO PETER, JAMES, AND JOHN

SCRIPTURE: MATTHEW 17

PART 1

CONTEXT

Before you begin your study, we will start with the context of the story we are about to read together: the setting, both cultural and historical; the people involved; and where our passage fits in the larger setting of Scripture. All these things help us make sense of what we're reading. Understanding the context of a Bible story is fundamental to reading Scripture well. Getting your bearings before you read will enable you to answer the question *What am I about to read?*

REV. DR. JOANN HUMMEL likes to joke that she'd never even climbed a tree before she set out to climb Mount Kilimanjaro, Africa's tallest mountain.[1] She was fifty-four years old—with two arthroscopic knee surgeries under her caps—when the mission of the Freedom Challenge[2] compelled her to hike eight days to the summit of what she now affectionately refers to as "Kili."

I didn't understand why she would go eight days without a shower or wake up at midnight, every night, to hike for hours in freezing temperatures—until JoAnn explained that her adventure would raise money for the rescue and rehabilitation of trafficked people. She was on a mission.

The sheer achievement and the important cause would have been joy enough. And summitting Kilimanjaro created a lifelong bond among the women in her hiking group, producing stories they will relive until glory. But JoAnn also delighted in a deeply personal experience with God on Mount Kilimanjaro—an encounter forged in adversity that fundamentally changed her perspective.

As you climb nineteen thousand feet up the largest freestanding mountain in the world, the air gets thin. *Real thin.* The higher you go, JoAnn explained, the less you can talk because you have to focus on your breathing; oxygen is harder to come by with each step. Concentrating only on the air drawing in and out of her lungs sustained her when the mountain's terrain felt impossible. With each labored inhale and exhale, Pastor JoAnn began to understand what it means that God is closer than our breath.

I would have been scared out of my mind doing what JoAnn did. When I told her this, she said, "The fear was real, but Jesus was close." And isn't this profound wisdom for how you and I can process the fears of life? When your life feels like an impossibly high mountain to climb, and when you are winded from adversity, Jesus can calm your fears with his nearness. He is as close to you as your own breath. JoAnn set out to climb in solidarity with human-trafficking victims and raise awareness of their plight, and she accomplished her goals. But she also cultivated hope in adversity, a skill we could all stand to develop.

In our study this week, we are going to see another group of people climbing a mountain and gasping through adversity. The Transfiguration was the mountain-top experience where Jesus showed Peter, James, and John how to deal with distressing circumstances—with a glimpse of Christ's future glory.

I know you might be in one of life's snowstorms right now, or maybe your story is paused on a massive cliff-hanger. Hang on a bit longer. The way Jesus encourages his disciples will bolster your faith.

As JoAnn watched her exhales freeze in the air right in front of her eyes, she was reminded that her Creator, the One who gives her breath, was accompanying her journey. It is a memorable moment in her faith walk that she loves to share about all these years later. Peter, James, and John experienced something similar in Matthew 17 on the Mount of Transfiguration. They, too, were scared—but witnessed a "moment of divine disclosure" with Jesus that helped them see past their present and into their hopeful future.[3]

Ever since the fall from Mount Eden, God's people have been trying to reverse the point of "no coming back" and inch closer to God's presence. By his grace, God keeps regathering and redeeming us, like he did for the Israelites on Mount Sinai. And he keeps bringing us back to himself, closer and closer, first at Sinai and then again through Jesus' incarnation, his embodied presence on earth.

In our last lesson, we zeroed in on Jesus' teaching in his Sermon on the Mount. In this sermon of all sermons, Jesus showed his disciples what Kingdom living looks like. Jesus ascended that mountain to show us a new way to live: wholeheartedly. The fact that Jesus can be seen on these mountains in Matthew's Gospel is a signal that God is getting closer to us. The Sinai people could only hear God's voice and hope that Moses was mediating well on their behalf, through the clouds, at the top of the mountain. That Jesus brought the people *with him* up the mountainside for the Sermon on the Mount represents the move Jesus is making to help us, metaphorically speaking, get back up to an Eden where we can enjoy God's presence fully.

If Mount Eden was about being exiled from God's presence and Mount Sinai about getting back to the foot of the mountain, where God was appearing, then the Sermon on the Mount is about going up the side of the mountain *with God*, and the Transfiguration is about seeing God's glory at the top. The whole Bible points us to the summit of God himself; in the end, Mount Zion is where all believers will be gathered with God to enjoy the new heaven and new earth.

Six days before Jesus' transfiguration, he'd been teaching his disciples about his upcoming death. Can you imagine how alarming that would have been for Jesus' disciples? Although Peter had just confessed his faith in Jesus as Messiah, none of the disciples could comprehend how much Jesus' kingship was going to cost him, let alone what it would cost *them*. The Cross would come before glory.

Jesus' actions on the Mount of Transfiguration were meant to help his disciples process the troubling announcement of his death and the intimidating truth that followers of Jesus need to deny themselves and take up their cross to truly be Christ followers. Just as Christ's disciples were beginning to grasp that he was fulfilling the laws of the Torah, he showed them he was fulfilling the prophets, too.

1. **PERSONAL CONTEXT: What is going on in your life right now that might impact how you understand this Bible story?**

2. **SPIRITUAL CONTEXT: If you've never studied this Bible story before, what piques your curiosity? If you've studied this passage before, what are some things you remember being taught on the subject?**

PART 2

SEEING

Seeing the text is vital if we want the heart of the Scripture passage to sink in. We read slowly and intentionally through the text with the context in mind. As we practice close, thoughtful reading of Scripture, we pick up on phrases, implications, and meanings we might otherwise have missed. Part 2 includes close Scripture reading and observation questions to empower you to answer the question *What is the story saying?*

1. **Fill out the conversation bubbles of Jesus' conversation with Peter as you read Matthew 16:21-28:**

[21] From that time on Jesus began to explain to his disciples that he must go to Jerusalem and suffer many things at the hands of the elders, the chief priests and the teachers of the law, and that he must be killed and on the third day be raised to life.

[22] Peter took him aside and began to rebuke him. "Never, Lord!" he said. "This shall never happen to you!"

[23] Jesus turned and said to Peter, "Get behind me, Satan! You are a stumbling block to me; you do not have in mind the concerns of God, but merely human concerns."

[24] Then Jesus said to his disciples, "Whoever wants to be my disciple must deny themselves and take up their cross and follow me. [25] For

whoever wants to save their life will lose it, but whoever loses their life for me will find it. ²⁶ What good will it be for someone to gain the whole world, yet forfeit their soul? Or what can anyone give in exchange for their soul? ²⁷ For the Son of Man is going to come in his Father's glory with his angels, and then he will reward each person according to what they have done.

²⁸ "Truly I tell you, some who are standing here will not taste death before they see the Son of Man coming in his kingdom."

MATTHEW 16:21-28

Peter's rebuke in Matthew 16:22

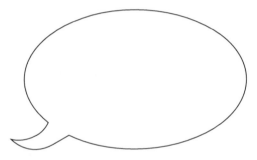

Jesus' rebuke in Matthew 16:23

2. According to Matthew 16:21, what prompted Peter to rebuke Jesus?

Can you imagine reprimanding Jesus? I can't . . . and can. I'd never say something like this out loud to Jesus' face, but I'd think it for sure. Jesus' announcement of his death really set Peter off, and for good reason. Jesus' disciples had turned their whole lives upside down to join God's mission, and they were all expecting action—a coup or a holy war to drive the Roman Empire from their homeland. But Jesus was going to inaugurate his Kingdom of peace through personal sacrifice on the cross and then invite his disciples—which includes all of us—to follow his cruciform way of living.

3. **According to Matthew 16:23, what did Jesus call Peter, and why was Jesus so mad at Peter?**

This one had to wound Peter's ego. Jesus called him evil. Apparently, denying Jesus' death on the cross was a work of Satan.

4. **In your own words, summarize what Jesus told his followers about discipleship in Matthew 16:24-26.**

   ▲

   ▲

   ▲

   ▲

Joining God's mission is nothing like becoming a member of a social club. Being in on Christ's mission means radical allegiance to the way of Christ, which includes a life committed to self-denial and a willingness to lose it all.

5. **Read Matthew 17:1-9, circling every time there is a comment or allusion of light below:**

17 After six days Jesus took with him Peter, James and John the brother of James, and led them up a high mountain by themselves. [2] There he was transfigured before them. His face shone like the sun, and his clothes became as white as the light. [3] Just then there appeared before them Moses and Elijah, talking with Jesus.

[4] Peter said to Jesus, "Lord, it is good for us to be here. If you wish, I will put up three shelters—one for you, one for Moses and one for Elijah."

[5] While he was still speaking, a bright cloud covered them, and a voice from the cloud said, "This is my Son, whom I love; with him I am well pleased. Listen to him!"

[6] When the disciples heard this, they fell facedown to the ground, terrified. [7] But Jesus came and touched them. "Get up," he said. "Don't be afraid." [8] When they looked up, they saw no one except Jesus.

[9] As they were coming down the mountain, Jesus instructed them, "Don't tell anyone what you have seen, until the Son of Man has been raised from the dead."

MATTHEW 17:1-9

6. **According to Matthew 17:1, Jesus' timing for the Transfiguration followed something important six days earlier. What happened in Matthew 16:21?**

Peter, James, and John must have been on high alert with the news that Jesus would not just die eventually but would suffer at the hands of his political enemies and be killed. No wonder they were terrified. They were already unnerved by doom.

7. What are some reasons the disciples may have been terrified in Matthew 17:6?

▲

▲

▲

▲

Before we wrap up our close reading of the Transfiguration and the events surrounding this special moment, I want you to see the link between the special revelation given to Peter, James, and John in Matthew 17 and Jesus' baptism in Matthew 3. The two scenes have several things in common, including the heavens opening up and the voice of the Father affirming Jesus' identity as God's Son. Both theophanies, or appearances of God, use similar words—God essentially repeats what he said in Matthew 3 in Matthew 17. The only difference is that on the Mount of Transfiguration, God adds a few extra words.

8. Let's look at how God the Father introduced Jesus on these two occasions.

JESUS' BAPTISM AND TRANSFIGURATION

Write out what God says about
Jesus in Matthew 3:17.

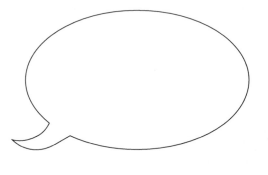

Write out what God says about
Jesus in Matthew 17:5 and
underline the bonus words.

9. Compare what God said in Matthew 3:17 and Matthew 17:5. Why do you think God added those words (underlined in the chart above)?

One of the ways we can grow hopeful when life is hard is to listen to Jesus. I know this sounds overly simplistic, but if I'm honest, I really struggle to listen to Jesus. In my life, his voice gets crowded out by all the Zoom meetings, chattering kiddos running through the house, Amazon Prime doorbell rings, and onslaught of advertisements coming my way through social media. Perhaps one of the reasons God positions the Transfiguration on a mountaintop is to move his disciples away from the noise and distractions of their lives . . . so they can pay attention to only his voice.

10. When do you hear Jesus' voice most clearly in your own life?

11. What crowds out his voice in your life?

PART 3

UNDERSTANDING

Now that we've finished a close reading of the Scriptures, we're going to spend some time on interpretation: doing our best to understand what God was saying to the original audience and what he's teaching us through the process. But to do so, we need to learn his ways and consider how God's Word would have been understood by the original audience before applying the same truths to our own lives. "Scripture interpretation" may sound a little stuffy, but understanding what God means to communicate to us in the Bible is crucial to enjoying a close relationship with Jesus. Part 3 will enable you to answer the question *What does it mean?*

I DON'T WANT YOU TO MISS THE SIGNIFICANCE of Moses and Elijah being present with Jesus for the Transfiguration. Just as the mountain backdrop is not random in the Bible, neither is God's invitation to two eminent figures from Israel's history, Moses and Elijah[4]: Moses represented the law, and Elijah represented the prophets.[5]

As Richard Bauckham so beautifully summarized in his book *Who Is God?*, we should begin to see some overlap between Jesus, Moses, and Elijah.[6] All of them faced bitter opposition to their ministries and lived through rejection and suffering. But Jesus stands apart as the One whose figure was transformed in front of Peter, James, and John. Jesus was the One identified by God as his Son. And Jesus alone went to the cross for our sins and was raised from the dead to conquer death.

Jesus has a lot in common with Moses and Elijah, but they are not equal. Jesus explained that he fulfilled the law and the prophets in the Sermon on the Mount, and now, in the Transfiguration, he proves it.

1. **If you are familiar with Moses' story in the Bible, what comes to mind first when you think of Moses? If you are not as familiar with Moses' story, look back at lesson two and pull out one thing you learned about him.**

2. **If you are familiar with Elijah's story in the Bible, what comes to mind first when you think of Elijah? If you are not as familiar with Elijah's story, look up 1 Kings 17 and write out one thing you learn about Elijah.**

MAKING CONNECTIONS

An important part of understanding the meaning of a Bible passage is getting a sense of its place in the broader storyline of Scripture. When we make connections between different parts of the Bible, we get a glimpse of the unity and cohesion of the Scriptures.

The Transfiguration provided Christ's disciples with a glimpse of his future glory, a glory that comes to fulfillment in the final New Testament book of the Bible, Revelation.[7] Revelation is written in a genre called apocalyptic literature and is a prophetic letter authored by the apostle John to the churches where he had been a leader. At times, the content of John's visions seems wild, but through it all is an encouragement to be faithful to Christ, knowing that he will be faithful to us. The glory Peter, James, and John peeked into at the Transfiguration finds its completion in the book of Revelation.

At the end of the book, in Revelation 21, an angel takes John somewhere special for a vision about the very end of God's Storyline Project (Revelation 21:9-14). You've got one guess where a vision of the new heaven and new earth are unveiled to John. *Yup*. A mountain. There on that final mountain, Mount Zion, God's presence shines in all its glory.

3. According to Revelation 21:23-25, what will not be needed in the final city of God?

On Mount Zion, you and I will live forever in God's presence. We won't need the sun or moon because Jesus is the lamp, or light, of the city. Night will cease to exist in the radiance of God's presence.

▲ ▲ ▲

Let's check back in on our Mountains Storyline.

THE MOUNTAINS STORYLINE OF SCRIPTURE

Location	God's Presence	Revelation
Mount Eden	walking among his people on the mountaintop	God is Creator.
Mount Sinai	descending from the mountaintop with strict parameters	God keeps covenants.
Mount of the Sermon	inviting his disciples to ascend the mountain with him	Jesus fulfills the law.
Mount of Transfiguration	talking with his disciples on top of the mountain	Christ is Messiah.
Mount of the Great Commission	commissioning his disciples to go down from the mountain to go and make disciples	Jesus is with us always.

God's People	Instruction	Identity
Adam and Eve	Do not eat from the Tree of Life.	We are made in God's image, created with purpose and dignity, fashioned to care for God's world and all people.
the Israelites	Obey God's laws.	God's people, the Israelites, the people he rescued and redeemed from slavery, are in a covenant relationship with him that will enable them to bea blessing to all people.
Christ followers	Internalize God's laws.	Christ followers, like the Israelites, are able to internalize God's laws through the power of the Holy Spirit and Christ's example. In doing so, we become a blessing to all people.
Peter, James, and John	Do not be afraid.	Christ followers can stay hopeful through hardship because after the Crucifixion is the Resurrection.
the disciples	Go and make disciples.	Christ followers are commissioned to carry out Jesus' mission but can only do so with Christ's presence.

1. **Where in your life do you need the special, concentrated presence of God?**

2. **What did you learn about God's character in this lesson?**

3. **How should these truths shape your faith community and change you?**

RESPONDING

The purpose of Bible study is to help you become more Christlike; that's why part 4 will include journaling space for your reflection on and responses to the content and a blank checklist for actionable next steps. You'll be able to process what you're learning so that you can live out the concepts and pursue Christlikeness. Part 4 will enable you to answer the questions *What truths is this passage teaching?* and *How do I apply this to my life?*

SOME OF MY FRIENDS who have been pastored or mentored by JoAnn, the Mount Kilimanjaro climber, call her their "ministry godmother" or the "pastors' pastor." And I can confirm that both titles are accurate. Ever the shepherd of those she leads, JoAnn wrote devotionals for her Freedom Challenge climbing group. *Of course she did.* One of her Mount Kilimanjaro devotionals happened to be a teaching on Jesus' transfiguration.

Here is her Transfiguration takeaway: Jesus wants to transfigure *you*.

Jesus desires for you and me to be changed by his revelation and then, JoAnn says, take our "newly given clarity back to the people and lives given to us."

You probably have a God story or two you retell often when sharing about your faith. For Peter, James, and John, Jesus' change in appearance would certainly be one such story. I'm convinced that Peter, James, and John were themselves transfigured at the Transfiguration—because their lives and writings show that they gained a supernatural hope to carry on when life got hard.

1. JESUS' TRANSFIGURATION CULTIVATED HOPE IN PETER.

In 1 Peter 2:9, Peter says that Christ followers are called out of darkness and into God's marvelous light, and I think this could be an allusion to the Transfiguration. As Peter was called out of a shadow of grief and into his bright future, so, too, should we take Jesus up on his invitation to leave gloom for glory.

The story of the Transfiguration is a critical feature of Peter's whole second book in the New Testament, 2 Peter. All these years later in Peter's life, he can't help but retell the gripping Transfiguration story—but this time, he offers application for all his readers, and ultimately, for us.

> 16 **We did not follow cleverly devised myths when we made known to you the power and coming of our Lord Jesus Christ, but we had been eyewitnesses of his majesty.** 17 **For he received honor and glory from God the Father when that voice was conveyed to him by the Majestic Glory, saying, "This is my Son, my Beloved, with whom I am well pleased."** 18 **We ourselves heard this voice come from heaven, while we were with him on the holy mountain.**
>
> 19 **So we have the prophetic message more fully confirmed. You will do well to be attentive to this as to a lamp shining in a dark place, until the day dawns and the morning star rises in your hearts.**
>
> 2 PETER 1:16-19, NRSV

2. JESUS' TRANSFIGURATION CULTIVATED HOPE IN JAMES.

While the New Testament doesn't include any letters written by James (at least, not the James who witnessed the Transfiguration), we do catch a glimpse of him in the book of Acts, and what we see is deeply moving: James was the first of Jesus' disciples to give up his life for the sake of the gospel (Acts 12:1-2). James had the benefit of witnessing the glorious luminosity of God's presence in real time with

Jesus in the flesh, and it left him with the radical hope that he would experience that glory again on the other side of even the deepest darkness.

3. JESUS' TRANSFIGURATION CULTIVATED HOPE IN JOHN.

John gets straight to the point when repurposing his Transfiguration testimony in his first letter. He simply says, "God is light" (1 John 1:5). In the second chapter of 1 John, John uses light and darkness as a metaphor for our relationship with God. To be in the light is to obey God's all-important command to love one another, and to live in darkness is to ignore God's mission to love. The bright spot with Jesus on the Mount of Transfiguration became a filter for John's writing.

John never got over the Transfiguration. That much is clear from his final writing project, the book of Revelation. John paints a picture with his words to show us that the glimpse of glory on the Mount of Transfiguration pales in comparison to the night-free living you and I will experience in the new heaven and new earth.

▲ ▲ ▲

You know what all these men had in common besides being on the Mount of Transfiguration? All of them suffered hardship after Christ's ascension. We already know from Acts that James met his death in the early years of the church, and the book of Revelation opens with John as a prisoner on a rocky island. Stories passed down through the ages tell us that Peter, too, died a martyr's death. What kept them going? How did they put one foot in front of the other when their faith journey was a steep climb? They meditated on Jesus' nearness. They could do so because they witnessed Jesus' transformation on the Mount of Transfiguration.

What about you? Where is hope missing in your life? What challenges keep stealing your hope? Jesus' transfiguration provides us a pathway to hope when times are tough. That's what it did for Peter, James, and John. And that's what the Mount of Transfiguration can do for you, too.

Use this journaling space to process what you are learning.

Ask yourself how these truths impact your relationship with God and with others.

What is the Holy Spirit bringing to your mind as actionable next steps in your faith journey?

▲

▲

▲

RELYING ON GOD'S PRESENCE TO CARRY YOU THROUGH

**MOUNT OF THE GREAT COMMISSION:
WHERE JESUS COMMISSIONS HIS DISCIPLES**

SCRIPTURE: MATTHEW 28

PART 1

CONTEXT

Before you begin your study, we will start with the context of the story we are about to read together: the setting, both cultural and historical; the people involved; and where our passage fits in the larger setting of Scripture. All these things help us make sense of what we're reading. Understanding the context of a Bible story is fundamental to reading Scripture well. Getting your bearings before you read will enable you to answer the question *What am I about to read?*

YOU MAY RECALL when I talked about my climb—*ahem*, I mean, walk—down Angel Fire mountain in our first lesson together. The ride on the ski lift up the mountain was beautiful, but I didn't mention that I grumbled and complained back down the slopes. It wasn't just that I was afraid of heights or that I didn't dress appropriately for the many scrapes and scratches, although both would be reason enough to make anyone a testy fuss-muss. And it wasn't because I wore slippery-soled shoes that, following a brief hailstorm, squeezed out mud with every step. *Nope.* Those were all contributing factors, but the main reason I struggled down Angel Fire was because I felt so inexperienced. Self-reliance wasn't an option.

Truth be told, I prefer the autonomy of self-sufficiency. It's just the way I'm wired. Maybe I'm speaking your truth, too, or describing one of your loved ones.

Perhaps you know what it's like to swat away a helping hand in pursuit of wobbly independence or to watch someone else do it.

But we're not built for self-reliance. Self-reliance is always going to get in the way of our relationship with God.

I think we know this deep down, but in practice, we struggle to appreciate our neediness and choose desperate dependence upon Christ.

The friends with us at Angel Fire—Shaun, Abby, and their three kids—live on the side of a cliff in Africa. Every single day of their lives as missionaries includes scaling steep terrain. As you can imagine, their family considered the beginner-level trail at Angel Fire mountain a walk in the park compared to their routes back home. Shaun used to be a wilderness guide, for climb's sake. He could have walked down Angel Fire backward with a blindfold faster than I could on my very best, bravest day.

As for my family, my son, Caleb, was fearlessly trailing his friends and laughing the whole way down while my husband, Aaron, was deep in conversation with Shaun, hiking carefree. I, on the other hand, looked like an obstinate, frightened mule being tugged down the mountain one yank at a time. And sounded just as annoying.

At one point, I refused a steep step in my struggle-climb, and Aaron offered his hand. "I'm right here," he said. Which is just what I needed to hear. I mean, I knew he was right next to me, but hearing the words was a comfort. I was relieved but still reluctant. I needed Aaron's and the rest of our group's presence to strengthen my fragile confidence. Even with their abiding presence, my faith was mixed with doubt in every step.

My experience at Angel Fire illustrates the wrestling we do as Christians when faith and doubt are both tugging at us. The Christian life is an ongoing tussle between hope and doubt, self-reliance and dependence on God, resisting our limitations and grasping a helping hand.

Our final lesson together is for the doubters. The Christians overwhelmed and defeated by their high calling—radical obedience to Jesus. I'd venture to say, if the Christian endeavor doesn't feel weighty, you might not understand the scope of the project. Self-reliance is not an option when it comes to making disciples of all nations or baptizing and teaching a whole generation a new way to live. If you are devoted to the church's mission—to bless the whole world—but find the sheer magnitude of this special assignment daunting, this lesson is for you.

If you hear nothing else in the *Mountains* study, hear this: *You are not alone.*

Yes, we have each other, and that will help, but our real, truest companion through all life's ups and downs will always be Jesus. His divine presence is a promise and the only thing powerful enough to pin our wandering hearts—while at the same time reaching the whole world with his love.

You will never be alone because Jesus is always with you.

In our Scripture passage this week, you and I are going to find a group of inexperienced Christ followers struggling to find a way down from the high of Jesus' resurrection. They, too, found themselves wrestling with mixed emotions—joy and fear, faith and doubt. They were confident Jesus was alive after his death and were filled with adoration . . . but also uncertain about what would happen next.

These men and women had been healed by Jesus, followed him through his three years of ministry, lived through the terror of his crucifixion, felt the agony of his three days in the tomb, and then experienced the jubilation of his resurrection. Talk about emotional whiplash.

What you are about to read is the conclusion of Matthew's Gospel, the eyewitness account of Jesus' life, death, and resurrection from Matthew's perspective. Matthew ends his Gospel with Jesus' parting words to his disciples before he ascended to the right hand of the Father. What you will see is that Jesus chose to use this final moment with his disciples to equip them with a vision of his glory and confirmation of his deity. Jesus' followers were sent out with the most powerful resource possible: the "reassuring promise of divine presence."[1]

On the final mountain in Matthew's Gospel, Jesus gathered and commissioned all his disciples, men and women, and set in motion the culmination of God's original plan detailed on Mount Eden—to see the whole world flourish.

1. **PERSONAL CONTEXT: What is going on in your life right now that might impact how you understand this Bible story?**

2. **SPIRITUAL CONTEXT: If you've never studied this Bible story before, what piques your curiosity? If you've studied this passage before, what are some things you remember being taught on the subject?**

PART 2

SEEING

Seeing the text is vital if we want the heart of the Scripture passage to sink in. We read slowly and intentionally through the text with the context in mind. As we practice close, thoughtful reading of Scripture, we pick up on phrases, implications, and meanings we might otherwise have missed. Part 2 includes close Scripture reading and observation questions to empower you to answer the question *What is the story saying?*

---

1. **Read Matthew 28:1–20, underlining all the emotions alluded to or described. If you are good at drawing emojis, use the margin to illustrate all the emotions in this passage too.**

28 After the Sabbath, at dawn on the first day of the week, Mary Magdalene and the other Mary went to look at the tomb.

² There was a violent earthquake, for an angel of the Lord came down from heaven and, going to the tomb, rolled back the stone and sat on it.
³ His appearance was like lightning, and his clothes were white as snow.
⁴ The guards were so afraid of him that they shook and became like dead men.

⁵ The angel said to the women, "Do not be afraid, for I know that you are looking for Jesus, who was crucified. ⁶ He is not here; he has risen, just

as he said. Come and see the place where he lay. [7] Then go quickly and tell his disciples: 'He has risen from the dead and is going ahead of you into Galilee. There you will see him.' Now I have told you."

[8] So the women hurried away from the tomb, afraid yet filled with joy, and ran to tell his disciples. [9] Suddenly Jesus met them. "Greetings," he said. They came to him, clasped his feet and worshiped him. [10] Then Jesus said to them, "Do not be afraid. Go and tell my brothers to go to Galilee; there they will see me."

[11] While the women were on their way, some of the guards went into the city and reported to the chief priests everything that had happened. [12] When the chief priests had met with the elders and devised a plan, they gave the soldiers a large sum of money, [13] telling them, "You are to say, 'His disciples came during the night and stole him away while we were asleep.' [14] If this report gets to the governor, we will satisfy him and keep you out of trouble." [15] So the soldiers took the money and did as they were instructed. And this story has been widely circulated among the Jews to this very day.

[16] Then the eleven disciples went to Galilee, to the mountain where Jesus had told them to go. [17] When they saw him, they worshiped him; but some doubted. [18] Then Jesus came to them and said, "All authority in heaven and on earth has been given to me. [19] Therefore go and make disciples of all nations, baptizing them in the name of the Father and of the Son and of the Holy Spirit, [20] and teaching them to obey everything I have commanded you. And surely I am with you always, to the very end of the age."

MATTHEW 28:1-20

I've always envied Peter, James, and John's experience in Matthew 17, when Jesus transforms before their eyes and gives a preview of his post-Resurrection glory. It would have been incredible to see women included in that trusted small group at the Transfiguration. Not until my research for this study did I catch that a group of women have their own Transfiguration-like experience right before the Great Commission.

2. **Write out what the angel says to the terrified women to comfort them at the empty tomb in Matthew 28:5:**

What a comfort the angel provides to the women. That's exactly what I would have needed to hear too. I'm imagining the women out of breath, with tears streaming down their faces and their hearts pumping through their chests as they search for their missing Savior. And I'm envisioning their relief as soon as the angel says, "Do not be afraid."

3. **According to Matthew 28:8, what two emotions did the women feel after being sent by Jesus to tell their brothers he is risen?**

☐ joy
☐ exhaustion
☐ fear
☐ frustration

What a combo. Joy and fear together remind me of riding a roller coaster. You have that rush screaming down a sharp turn and the joy of your hair moving through the wind.

4. **According to Matthew 28:17, what two emotions did the male disciples feel after seeing that Jesus had risen from the dead?**

    ☐ adoration
    ☐ relief
    ☐ doubt
    ☐ annoyance

As biblical scholar Jeannine K. Brown and theologian Kyle Roberts so poetically describe in their commentary on Matthew, over and over Matthew's Gospel shows us how, after divine revelation, Jesus' disciples both "worship and waver."[2] This should bring you comfort. You can worship God sincerely *and* struggle with a wavering faith because "doubt and fidelity to the mission of Jesus are not mutually exclusive."[3] I know I do. I'm writing this Bible study fully confident that Jesus is alive and his mission is unstoppable. But I'm also battling fear. The good news is that worship and doubt can coexist. In fact, I would argue that we have to have at least a little doubt to exercise faith.

5. **Write out Jesus' Great Commission to his disciples in your own words based on Matthew 28:18-20:**

"Surely I am with you always, to the very end of the age." Like a loud, rhythmic drumbeat, God's presence is the pulse of the Bible. Notice with me how consistently Scripture pulses with the Lord's abiding presence.

According to Genesis 3:8, where was God on Mount Eden?

According to Genesis 28:12-17, what did God promise in Jacob's dream at Bethel?

According to Genesis 35:2-3, what did Jacob say about God's presence?

According to Genesis 39:20-23, why was Joseph successful?

According to Exodus 3:12, what did God say to Moses about being insecure about his calling to go up against Pharaoh and lead the Israelites out of slavery?

According to Joshua 1:8-9, what did God say to Joshua about being afraid and discouraged?

According to 2 Samuel 7:9, what did God say is the reason David and the Israelites had survived their enemies' attacks?

According to Jeremiah 1:4-8, what did God promise to the prophet Jeremiah when he resisted his calling?

Fellow doubters, take heart. A burden to live into your calling doesn't have to feel like a boulder. Instead, it could be an opportunity to enjoy the nearness of your Savior. He is with us.

PART 3

UNDERSTANDING

Now that we've finished a close reading of the Scriptures, we're going to spend some time on interpretation: doing our best to understand what God was saying to the original audience and what he's teaching us through the process. But to do so, we need to learn his ways and consider how God's Word would have been understood by the original audience before applying the same truths to our own lives. "Scripture interpretation" may sound a little stuffy, but understanding what God means to communicate to us in the Bible is crucial to enjoying a close relationship with Jesus. Part 3 will enable you to answer the question *What does it mean?*

IN THE SAME WAY I began and ended this Bible study with my Angel Fire story, the apostle Matthew used Jesus' presence as a bookend for his book, the Gospel of Matthew. You've just read the end of Matthew's historical biography of Jesus' life, death, and resurrection. Now flip all the way back to the beginning of Matthew's Gospel to see how this all ties together.

1. **Read Matthew 1:18-23, underlining every reference to Jesus.**

> [18] Now the birth of Jesus the Messiah took place in this way. When his mother Mary had been engaged to Joseph, but before they lived together, she was found to be with child from the Holy Spirit. [19] Her husband Joseph, being a righteous man and unwilling to expose her to public disgrace, planned to dismiss her quietly. [20] But just when he had

resolved to do this, an angel of the Lord appeared to him in a dream and said, "Joseph, son of David, do not be afraid to take Mary as your wife, for the child conceived in her is from the Holy Spirit. ²¹ She will bear a son, and you are to name him Jesus, for he will save his people from their sins." ²² All this took place to fulfill what had been spoken by the Lord through the prophet:

²³ "Look, the virgin shall conceive and bear a son,
    and they shall name him Emmanuel,"

which means, "God is with us."

MATTHEW 1:18-23, NRSV

2. **What do you think Matthew accomplishes by emphasizing God's identity as the One who is with us in both the first and the last chapters of his Gospel?**

No one says it better than Richard B. Hays in *Echoes of the Scriptures in the Gospels*:

Jesus—who even before his birth was identified by Matthew the Evangelist as Emmanuel, God with us—now speaks after his resurrection in fulfillment of precisely that identity. He possesses all authority in heaven and on earth, and he promises his sustaining presence throughout all time in all places, as he sends his followers out to summon all nations to obey him.[4]

Why does the Great Commission take place on a mountain? Because God uses mountains in the Bible to symbolize places where we can enjoy his presence always. Even if we rebel against God and reject his presence, he's proven to us through Mount Eden that he will still come close to us. Even if we fail to fulfill his laws for us the way the Israelites failed to follow the Torah, God has proven to us through Mount Sinai that he will be with us no matter what. Even if our hearts need an overhaul, like the people listening to Jesus' Sermon on the Mount, God promises to renovate our hearts from the inside out. Even if we need to be transformed into Christ's likeness, like Peter, James, and John did at the Mount of Transfiguration, God will do it on our behalf so that we can be close to him and become more like him.

Which brings us to our final mountain, the Mount of the Great Commission. If we had any doubts that God's presence is faltering, if we had any concerns that we are too far gone, God reminds us at the Mount of the Great Commission: He will be with us always.

MAKING CONNECTIONS

An important part of understanding the meaning of a Bible passage is getting a sense of its place in the broader storyline of Scripture. When we make connections between different parts of the Bible, we get a glimpse of the unity and cohesion of the Scriptures.

Reading Bible stories set on mountaintops for the past several weeks has enabled us to read previous peaks in God's story of grace retrospectively. Through this study, you've connected Mount Eden to Mount Sinai to the Mount of the Sermon to the Mount of Transfiguration and now to the Mount of the Great Commission. And how are they all connected? They are all pointing us to Jesus.

Christ is the redemption of Adam and Eve's rebellion on Mount Eden. He is the fulfillment of Israel's laws at Mount Sinai. With that in mind, notice with me how connected the Great Commission is to other mountaintop stories that happen earlier in our faith history: namely, the giving of the law at Mount Sinai

(Exodus 19–20) and the Transfiguration, where Christ reveals his glory to Peter, James, and John (Matthew 17).

3. **Compare Matthew 28:16-20 to Exodus 19:16-18. List out everything these two mountaintop scenes have in common.**

▲

▲

▲

JESUS' GREAT COMMISSION AND
THE GIVING OF THE LAW AT MOUNT SINAI

Matthew 28:16-20 (The Great Commission)	Exodus 19:16-18 (At Mount Sinai)

We can assume that the original audience learning from Matthew's Gospel would have instinctively remembered the law-giving scene from Mount Sinai and started to connect the two milestone moments to each other. These kinds of sacred echoes in the text can serve to strengthen our faith in Christ. Jesus is the new Moses—but he is much more than a great leader or arbiter of truth. Jesus *is* truth. And he doesn't need a go-between to communicate with us. He comes close and will stay forever.

▲ ▲ ▲

Let's check back in on our Mountains Storyline.

THE MOUNTAINS STORYLINE OF SCRIPTURE

Location	God's Presence	Revelation
Mount Eden	walking among his people on the mountaintop	God is Creator.
Mount Sinai	descending from the mountaintop with strict parameters	God keeps covenants.
Mount of the Sermon	inviting his disciples to ascend the mountain with him	Jesus fulfills the law.
Mount of Transfiguration	talking with his disciples on top of the mountain	Christ is Messiah.
Mount of the Great Commission	commissioning his disciples to go down from the mountain to go and make disciples	Jesus is with us always.

God's People	Instruction	Identity
Adam and Eve	Do not eat from the Tree of Life.	We are made in God's image, created with purpose and dignity, fashioned to care for God's world and all people.
the Israelites	Obey God's laws.	God's people, the Israelites, the people he rescued and redeemed from slavery, are in a covenant relationship with him that will enable them to bea blessing to all people.
Christ followers	Internalize God's laws.	Christ followers, like the Israelites, are able to internalize God's laws through the power of the Holy Spirit and Christ's example. In doing so, we become a blessing to all people.
Peter, James, and John	Do not be afraid.	Christ followers can stay hopeful through hardship because after the Crucifixion is the Resurrection.
the disciples	Go and make disciples.	Christ followers are commissioned to carry out Jesus' mission but can only do so with Christ's presence.

1. Where in your life do you need the special, concentrated presence of God?

2. What did you learn about God's character in this lesson?

3. How should these truths shape your faith community and change you?

RESPONDING

The purpose of Bible study is to help you become more Christlike; that's why part 4 will include journaling space for your reflection on and responses to the content and a blank checklist for actionable next steps. You'll be able to process what you're learning so that you can live out the concepts and pursue Christlikeness. Part 4 will enable you to answer the questions *What truths is this passage teaching?* and *How do I apply this to my life?*

EACH AND EVERY PART of the *Mountains* study changed my life, but this lesson is going to stay with me forever (pun intended). As I researched the Great Commission, I had to pause to absorb Ian Boxall's phrase "the God who stays."[5] Let that sink in for a moment. Our God is the One who stays. Unlike the relationships that left us feeling abandoned, forgotten, or unimportant, Jesus cannot and will not leave us. To anyone with a self-protecting guard around their heart, you are safe with Jesus. He is the One who will stay always.

As the Great Commission started to settle into my soul, these words of comfort came to mind:

1. YOU ARE NOT ALONE.

And maybe that's what you ache to hear—that you are not alone. I have godly men and women in my orbit who have suffered the agonizing loneliness that comes after being left at the altar, abandoned in hardship, rejected by a loved one, let go from a job, or fired from a church. As the world closes in, we start to look around and feel utterly alone. But that's not the whole truth. Yes, you may be standing by yourself or facing the unthinkable without the people you thought would always be by your side, but you are not without a companion. Jesus is with you.

2. YOU ARE NOT DOING GOD'S WORK ALONE.

If you are on mission for Jesus, you can't do that work without God's help. Self-reliance can be popular, a celebrated sign of ability and aptitude—but it doesn't translate to ministry success. Quite the opposite. When Jesus commissions Christians to go and make disciples of all nations—to bless everyone with the gift of his teaching and the opportunity to express their faith in baptism—he's not encouraging us to get out there and get things done *on our own*. Your mission to share God's love can't be separated from his staying presence. Why? Because without Jesus' presence, we are just peddling ourselves or our stories. And yes, our stories are powerful testimonies of God's work in our lives. Please keep sharing your story. It matters. Yes, giving ourselves away to good causes has benefits and value. But there's a way to serve God where Jesus becomes auxiliary to the efforts. Jesus' calling on our lives, to invite everyone into a relationship with him, isn't something we can do alone. He has to be with us. And the good news is that he is.

▲ ▲ ▲

In Jesus' final mountaintop meeting with his disciples, he commissions worshipful and doubtful Christians with the promise of his staying presence. In doing so, he gives permission to folks like you and me, who process conflicting feelings in our faith, to rely on Jesus' divine presence.

In much the same way that Aaron offered me his hand on Angel Fire mountain and said, "I'm right here," Jesus is doing the same for you.

Use this journaling space to process what you are learning.

Ask yourself how these truths impact your relationship with God and with others.

What is the Holy Spirit bringing to your mind as actionable next steps in your faith journey?

- ▲
- ▲
- ▲

As You Go

YOU DID IT. You study-climbed five mountain peaks in the Bible: Mount Eden, Mount Sinai, the Mount of the Sermon, the Mount of Transfiguration, and the Mount of the Great Commission. All five mountaintop stories share several key elements:

- ▲ the special, concentrated presence of God;
- ▲ a history-changing revelation of God's character;
- ▲ the forming of a faith community or a people of faith; and
- ▲ important teaching or instructions from God about how to live his way.

These stand-out elements bring together a cohesive storyline (see pages 122–123).

With every mountain setting, I hope God reminded you that he has, and always will, make a way to meet with you. He loves to disclose and reveal his character to you. Getting close to you and staying close is his heartbeat.

Whether it's a spiritual mountaintop or a valley of doubt, there's no mountain too high or valley too low to keep you away from his love.

PS: I've loved this journey with you, and I hope you join me again—this time, for the *Valleys* study.

THE MOUNTAINS STORYLINE OF SCRIPTURE

Location	God's Presence	Revelation
Mount Eden	walking among his people on the mountaintop	God is Creator.
Mount Sinai	descending from the mountaintop with strict parameters	God keeps covenants.
Mount of the Sermon	inviting his disciples to ascend the mountain with him	Jesus fulfills the law.
Mount of Transfiguration	talking with his disciples on top of the mountain	Christ is Messiah.
Mount of the Great Commission	commissioning his disciples to go down from the mountain to go and make disciples	Jesus is with us always.

God's People	Instruction	Identity
Adam and Eve	Do not eat from the Tree of Life.	We are made in God's image, created with purpose and dignity, fashioned to care for God's world and all people.
the Israelites	Obey God's laws.	God's people, the Israelites, the people he rescued and redeemed from slavery, are in a covenant relationship with him that will enable them to bea blessing to all people.
Christ followers	Internalize God's laws.	Christ followers, like the Israelites, are able to internalize God's laws through the power of the Holy Spirit and Christ's example. In doing so, we become a blessing to all people.
Peter, James, and John	Do not be afraid.	Christ followers can stay hopeful through hardship because after the Crucifixion is the Resurrection.
the disciples	Go and make disciples.	Christ followers are commissioned to carry out Jesus' mission but can only do so with Christ's presence.

Each **Storyline Bible Study** is five lessons long and can be paired with its thematic partner for a seamless, ten-week study. Complement the *Mountains* study with

VALLEYS
FINDING COURAGE, CONVICTION, AND CONFIDENCE IN LIFE'S LOW POINTS

Valleys in the Bible have far more meaning than just as geographical markers or pins on an ancient map. In his literary genius, God repurposes valley settings throughout Scripture to signal tests of faith—and the deepening of confidence in the One who is with us in the valley.

LESSON ONE: Trusting God with Your Giant-Sized Doubts
Valley of Eshkol: Where Moses' Spies Scout the Promised Land
NUMBERS 13–14

LESSON TWO: Facing Your Battles with Courage and Conviction
Valley of Kishon: Where Deborah and Jael Defeat Their Enemy
JUDGES 4–5

LESSON THREE: Staying Brave When the Odds Are against You
Valley of Elah: Where David Fights Goliath
1 SAMUEL 17

LESSON FOUR: Resisting Fear When Your Life Bottoms Out
Valley of Death: Where God Comforts Scared People
PSALM 23

LESSON FIVE: Resurrecting Hope When Your Confidence in God Is Lost
Valley of Dry Bones: Where Ezekiel Prophesies Israel's Restoration
EZEKIEL 37

Learn more at thestorylineproject.com.

CP1821

Storyline Bible Studies

Each study follows people, places, or things throughout the Bible.
This approach allows you to see the cohesive storyline of Scripture
and appreciate the Bible as the literary masterpiece that it is.

**Access free resources to help you teach or
lead a small group at thestorylineproject.com.**

CP1816

Acknowledgments

WITHOUT MY FAMILY'S SUPPORT, the **Storyline Bible Studies** would just be a dream. I'm exceedingly grateful for a family that prays and cheers for me when I step out to try something new. To my husband, Aaron, son, Caleb, and mom, Noemi: You three sacrificed the most to ensure that I had enough time and space to write. Thank you. And to all my extended family: I know an army of Armstrongs was praying and my family in Austin was cheering me on to the finish line. Thank you.

To my ministry partners at the Polished Network, Integrus Leadership, and Dallas Bible Church: Linking arms with you made this project possible. I love doing Kingdom work with you.

NavPress and Tyndale teams: Thank you for believing in me. You wholeheartedly embraced the concept, and you've made this project better in every way possible. Special thanks to David Zimmerman, my amazing editor Caitlyn Carlson, Elizabeth Schroll, Olivia Eldredge, David Geeslin, and the entire editorial and marketing teams.

Jana Burson: You were the catalyst. Thank you.

Teresa Swanstrom Anderson: Thank you for connecting me with Caitlyn. You'll forever go down in history as the person who made my dreams come true.

All my friends rallied to pray for this project when I was stressed about the deadlines. Thank you. We did it! Without your intercession, these wouldn't be complete. I want to give special thanks to Lee, Sarah, Amy, Ashton, Tiffany, and Jenn for holding up my arms to complete the studies.

Resources for Deeper Study

OLD TESTAMENT

Bearing God's Name: Why Sinai Still Matters by Carmen Joy Imes

The Epic of Eden: A Christian Entry into the Old Testament by Sandra L. Richter

NEW TESTAMENT

Echoes of Scripture in the Gospels by Richard B. Hays

The Gospels as Stories: A Narrative Approach to Matthew, Mark, Luke, and John by Jeannine K. Brown

BIBLE STUDY

Commentary on the New Testament Use of the Old Testament, eds. G. K. Beale and D. A. Carson

Dictionary of Biblical Imagery, eds. Leland Ryken, James C. Wilhoit, and Tremper Longman III

The Drama of Scripture: Finding Our Place in the Biblical Story by Craig G. Bartholomew and Michael W. Goheen

From Beginning to Forever: A Study of the Grand Narrative of Scripture by Elizabeth Woodson

How (Not) to Read the Bible: Making Sense of the Anti-Women, Anti-Science, Pro-Violence, Pro-Slavery and Other Crazy Sounding Parts of Scripture by Dan Kimball

How to Read the Bible as Literature . . . and Get More Out of It by Leland Ryken

Literarily: How Understanding Bible Genres Transforms Bible Study by Kristie Anyabwile

The Mission of God: Unlocking the Bible's Grand Narrative by Christopher J. H. Wright

"Reading Scripture as a Coherent Story" by Richard Bauckham, in *The Art of Reading Scripture*, eds. Ellen F. Davis and Richard B. Hays

Reading While Black: African American Biblical Interpretation as an Exercise in Hope by Esau McCaulley

Read the Bible for a Change: Understanding and Responding to God's Word by Ray Lubeck

Scripture as Communication: Introducing Biblical Hermeneutics by Jeannine K. Brown

What Is the Bible and How Do We Understand It? by Dennis R. Edwards

Words of Delight: A Literary Introduction to the Bible by Leland Ryken

About the Author

KAT ARMSTRONG was born in Houston, Texas, where the humidity ruins her Mexi-German curls. She is a powerful voice in our generation as a sought-after Bible teacher. She holds a master's degree from Dallas Theological Seminary and is the author of *No More Holding Back*, *The In-Between Place*, and the **Storyline Bible Studies**. In 2008, Kat cofounded the Polished Network to embolden working women in their faith and work. Kat is pursuing a doctorate of ministry in New Testament context at Northern Seminary and is a board member of the Polished Network. She and her husband, Aaron, have been married for twenty years; live in Dallas, Texas, with their son, Caleb; and attend Dallas Bible Church, where Aaron serves as the lead pastor.

KATARMSTRONG.COM   THESTORYLINEPROJECT.COM
@KATARMSTRONG1   @THESTORYLINEPROJECT

Make peace with your past.
Find hope in the present.
Step into your future.

CP1818

Notes

LESSON ONE | BECOMING SECURE IN YOUR IDENTITY

1. Tim Mackie and Jon Collins, "Exile, Episode 3: Exile from the Cosmic Mountain," *BibleProject Podcast*, February 14, 2018, https://bibleproject.com/podcast/exile-cosmic-mountain.
2. L. Michael Morales, *The Tabernacle Pre-Figured: Cosmic Mountain Ideology in Genesis and Exodus* (Leuven, Belgium: Peeters, 2012), 1–2.
3. Morales, *Tabernacle Pre-Figured*, 7.
4. Walter Brueggemann, *Genesis: A Bible Commentary for Teaching and Preaching* (Atlanta: John Knox Press, 1982), part one, 17.
5. Dan Kimball, *How (Not) to Read the Bible: Making Sense of the Anti-Women, Anti-Science, Pro-Violence, Pro-Slavery and Other Crazy Sounding Parts of Scripture* (Grand Rapids, MI: Zondervan, 2020), 173.
6. Rodney S. Sadler Jr., "Genesis," in *The Africana Bible: Reading Israel's Scriptures from Africa and the African Diaspora*, ed. Hugh R. Page Jr. (Minneapolis: Fortress Press, 2010), 70.
7. Tremper Longman III and Raymond B. Dillard, *An Introduction to the Old Testament*, 2nd ed. (Grand Rapids, MI: Zondervan, 2006), 57.
8. Longman and Dillard, *Introduction to the Old Testament*, 57.
9. Kimball, *How (Not) to Read the Bible*, 175.
10. Brueggemann, *Genesis*, 24.
11. Dru Johnson, *The Universal Story: Genesis 1–11* (Bellingham, WA: Lexham Press, 2018), 51–52.
12. Johnson, *Universal Story*, 52.
13. Brueggemann, *Genesis*, 25.

LESSON TWO | BELIEVING GOD LOVES YOU NO MATTER WHAT

1. Carmen Joy Imes, *Bearing God's Name: Why Sinai Still Matters* (Downers Grove, IL: InterVarsity Press, 2019), 2.
2. Tremper Longman III and Raymond B. Dillard, *An Introduction to the Old Testament*, 2nd ed. (Grand Rapids, MI: Zondervan, 2006), 71.
3. Walter Brueggemann, *Sabbath as Resistance: Saying No to the Culture of Now* (Louisville: Westminster John Knox Press, 2014), 3.
4. Brueggemann, *Sabbath as Resistance*, 5.
5. Longman III and Dillard, *Introduction to the Old Testament*, 72.

6. Brueggemann, *Sabbath as Resistance*, 34.
7. Michael W. Goheen and Craig G. Bartholomew, *The True Story of the Whole World: Finding Your Place in the Biblical Drama*, rev. ed. (Grand Rapids, MI: Brazos Press, 2020), 46.
8. William Dumbrell, as quoted in Goheen and Bartholomew, *True Story*, 45.
9. Judy Fentress-Williams, "Exodus," in *The Africana Bible: Reading Israel's Scriptures from Africa and The African Diaspora*, ed. Hugh R. Page Jr. (Minneapolis: Fortress Press, 2010), 80.
10. Imes, *Bearing God's Name*, 35.
11. P.G. George and Paul Swarup, "Exodus," in *South Asia Bible Commentary*, ed. Brian Wintle (Grand Rapids, MI: Zondervan, 2015), 100.

LESSON THREE | RECONSTRUCTING YOUR FAITH IN AN AGE OF DECONSTRUCTION
1. Dallas Willard, *The Divine Conspiracy: Rediscovering Our Hidden Life in God* (London: William Collins, 2014), 161.
2. Willard, *The Divine Conspiracy*, 153.
3. Jonathan T. Pennington, *The Sermon on the Mount and Human Flourishing: A Theological Commentary* (Grand Rapids, MI: Baker Academic, 2017), 138.
4. Pennington, *Sermon on the Mount*, 139–140.
5. Ian Boxall, *Discovering Matthew: Content, Interpretation, Reception* (Grand Rapids, MI: Eerdmans, 2015), 46.
6. Boxall, *Discovering Matthew*, 57.
7. Terence L. Donaldson, *Jesus on the Mountain: A Study in Matthean Theology* (Sheffield, England: JSOT Press, 1985), xxii.
8. Amy-Jill Levine, *The Sermon on the Mount: A Beginner's Guide to the Kingdom of Heaven* (Nashville: Abington, 2020), xvi–xvii.
9. Tim Mackie, "Jesus and the Torah: Gospel of Matthew Part 6," June 4, 2018, in *Exploring My Strange Bible,* podcast, MP3 audio, 49:56, https://www.podcastrepublic.net/podcast/1271147429.

LESSON FOUR | GROWING HOPEFUL WHEN YOUR LIFE IS HARD
1. "Kilimanjaro," National Geographic, accessed July 22, 2021, https://www.nationalgeographic.org/encyclopedia/kilimanjaro.
2. See https://www.thefreedomchallenge.com/#intro.
3. Richard Bauckham, *Who Is God?: Key Moments of Biblical Revelation* (Grand Rapids, MI: Baker Academic, 2020), 99.
4. Bauckham, *Who Is God?*, 100.
5. Jeannine K. Brown and Kyle Roberts, *Matthew: Two Horizons New Testament Commentary* (Grand Rapids, MI: Eerdmans, 2018), 158.
6. Bauckham, *Who Is God?*, 100.
7. Amy-Jill Levine and Marc Zvi Brettler, *The Jewish Annotated New Testament*, 2nd ed., New Revised Standard Version (Oxford: Oxford University Press, 2017), 42.

LESSON FIVE | RELYING ON GOD'S PRESENCE TO CARRY YOU THROUGH
1. Richard B. Hays, *Echoes of Scripture in the Gospels* (Waco, TX: Baylor University Press, 2016), 174.
2. Jeannine K. Brown and Kyle Roberts, *Matthew: Two Horizons New Testament Commentary* (Grand Rapids, MI: Eerdmans, 2018), 262.
3. Amy-Jill Levine and Marc Zvi Brettler, *The Jewish Annotated New Testament*, 2nd ed., New Revised Standard Version (Oxford: Oxford University Press, 2017), 66.
4. Hays, *Echoes*, 174.
5. Ian Boxall, *Discovering Matthew: Content, Interpretation, Reception* (Grand Rapids, MI: Eerdmans, 2015), 174.